...to breed a noble horse is
to share with God one of
His mysteries. As well as
one of His delights.

Tom Lea

CARDENAS:
HORSES & HOME

by ROBERT VAVRA

Home Photography
WAYNE CHASAN

Equine Photographic Galleries
THOMAS KILPER
TOMAS MIČEK
TILL LESSER
ROBERT VAVRA

Epilogue
MERCEDES GONZÁLEZ CORT

EQUIVISION

For Miguel Angel and Carmen for the beauty you bring to all horse lovers, and with deepest gratitude from the photographers to whom you have so generously extended your help and hospitality, especially from the writer of these words.

Library of Congress Control Number: 2004105422

Vavra, Robert.
    Cardenas: Horses & Home/Robert Vavra
    ISBN 0-9711329-1-7

HAND BOUND

First Edition 1 2 3 4 5 6 7 8 9 10

CONCEIVED AND DESIGNED BY ROBERT VAVRA
www.robertvavra.com

Gold embosed cloth cover drawing: Roger Bansemer

Printed in Hong Kong by: South Sea International Press Ltd.
Address: 3/F., Yip Cheung Centre, 10 Fung Yip Street, Chaiwan, Hong Kong
Email: books@ssip.com.hk Fax: (852) 2558 1473

CONTENTS

Flowing manes, arched necks, power and grace in movement: the most beautiful horses in the world gallop my mind with the mention of the name Cárdenas.

Because of their handsomeness, athletic ability and noble temperaments, the stallions and mares of Cárdenas are found from Madrid to Hollywood, from Mexico City to London, from San Juan to Munich – wherever the finest of Spanish Horses are bred and ridden. These renowned equines originate from Écija, a town between Seville and Cordoba, where one can still find the authentic Andalusian charm and flavor that brought me to Spain in 1958.

But apart from horses bearing the brand ⌼, other images brighten my mind with the name Cárdenas, those of Miguel Ángel and his wife Maria del Carmen. Forged by a mutual passion for horses, our friendship transcends more than a quarter of a century.

It was in the late 1970s when a search for equine models for my books attracted my attention to the name Cárdenas as much as recently did the planet Mars when it was closest to the earth in 600,000 years – the brightest star in the night sky. Then when I began a quest for the most photogenic Spanish equines, "Cárdenas" was the most brilliant star among horses in the Spanish heavens and one of the three most prominent names among breeders of Andalusians in Spain. The ranch was then frequently the winner of the Champion of Champions Stallion award and the best breeding farm awards at Seville's annual International Purebred Spanish Horse Show at the Pineda Club.

Those were marvelous times when the exhibition's focus was on horses, horses and more horses. However, it is said that progress is not for romantics. Today the event has been converted into the sort of commercial spectacle where women's apparel, hunting attire, antiques and automobiles are also marketed in a mammoth horse show similar to the epic equine events held in Germany and the United States. Only the language spoken and breed of horses shown distinguish these exhibitions from one another.

But back to Miguel Ángel and how he and his horses came into my life and, in doing so, have been viewed universally wherever books are sold and seen. At one of those relatively intimate Pineda shows, I saw the most magnificent of white stallions. Vasallo was a Velázquez stud reincarnated, a stallion of a dream, the essence of what the word *horse* conjures up romantically and artistically. Also, it was obvious that he possessed in great abundance one of the most desired characteristics of the Andalusian: nobility. His flying mane, flashing eyes,

ÉCIJA FROM THE CÁRDENAS MOORISH TOWER

flaring nostrils and apparently fiery character were controlled by his naturally gentle temperament. In human terms, he would have been considered both a 'gentleman' and a 'gentle man,' two very different, but equally appealing, qualities.

Little did I know, when I first saw Vasallo the influence he and his owners would have on my life and work. How could I have then imagined he would appear on the covers of my books *Le Cheval Nu* (the French edition of *Equus*), *Robert Vavra's Classic Horses* and *El Caballo Español* (the Spanish Edition of *The Andalusian*), that his photograph would also appear in advertisements for Jordache and White Horse Whiskey, on calendar covers, wine bottles and designer shirts; that it would be cast in silver jewelry, appear on greeting cards, posters, fine-art gallery prints, crystal and in collectors' images for The Franklin Mint.

It would have then seemed equally impossible that, because of a broken camera, a single image of Vasallo would gross over one-half million dollars and indirectly lead me to the taking of another image which, larger than life-size, would gallop on immense billboards along the freeways of Hollywood, would cause Robert Redford to phone me to be his creative advisor on a film, and would appear on theater posters and on the covers of thousands of music CDs, as well as on the jackets of more than ten million books.

So, how did this series of events transpire? After I had seen Vasallo at Pineda, I was determined to photograph him for my first horse book, *Equus*. When I mentioned this to friend and distinguished horse breeder Paco Lazo, he said Miguel Ángel Cárdenas was his good friend and that he would phone him about my feelings for Vasallo and my desire to include him in a book.

Time passed and it was August when I went to see Miguel Ángel in Écija, then about an hour from where I lived in Seville. Écija, which is known for its lovely skyline dominated by eleven church spires, has also received attention and publicity thanks to the presence of its world-famous equines – those of Cárdenas.

After a brief meeting, Miguel Ángel said his horses were completely at the disposal of my camera and he would do everything possible to assist. "How many men do you need to help photograph Vasallo at liberty?" he asked. Where did I want to photograph the stallion and at what time of day? "Logistics are not a problem," he assured. It was only important that everything was at my disposal to allow the realization of the images I had in mind. It should be mentioned that Miguel Ángel had only seen two of my books, both done in black and white, *Iberia* with James Michener focusing mostly on people and architecture, and *Bulls of Iberia*, a study of the Spanish fighting bull. His offer to help seemed especially generous, since he had not seen a single equine image of mine.

It was decided to photograph Vasallo from a structure next to a tree giving the impression the camera was in the foliage. As we spoke, Miguel Ángel mentioned the nearby Military Stud Farm's bands of young stallions corralled together, and he suggested I might want to stop there when I returned to Écija. First, he would phone the officer in charge. Also, I had a letter from General Merry Gordon, telling about my project and indicating I was to be given assistance at the army stud farms under his command.

Several days later I returned with camera and film to Écija. Late in the afternoon of my arrival, because of Miguel Ángel's introduction, I was able to photograph an army stallion back-lit, dust blossoming from his hooves. Little importance was given to this image. The next afternoon I photographed Vasallo. Forty rolls of film – 1,440 images – were shot in an attempt to capture the stallion's magnificence against the going sun, his mane rising like a cresting wave at sea.

Thirty years ago, having little confidence in Spanish film-processing, I sent the undeveloped film to California. Weeks later, when I opened the returned box of film, all of the rolls – except that from the army stud – were totally black due to a camera malfunction.

A few days later, I returned to Écija to hopefully capture Vasallo's image in action through the repaired camera's lens. Then came the long wait for the film to reach California and the worry it would be lost in the post on its way there or back. But it did arrive, and among the transparencies were the images of Vasallo mentioned earlier, which would not only be seen on book covers, but in one-man museum exhibitions in Austria and the United States, as well as in almost one-hundred private gallery shows across America, from Manhattan to San Francisco.

So Vasallo's photos in the book would take their place among those of other equine stars and be with the presence of human stars on their coffee tables, including those of Robert Redford, Bo Derek, William Shatner, Linda Evans, Charlton Heston, Ursula Andress, Michael Douglas, and Candice Bergen. More important, Vasallo would be in the libraries and on the bookshelves of hundreds of thousands of ordinary people who passionately love horses.

And what of the unknown horse photographed because of Miguel Ángel's influence at the Écija Military Farm? He would first appear in a small image on page one of my book *Equus*, published in six languages, a *Time-Life* major book club selection. Then he would remain forgotten for years until Delacourt Press insisted on using his image on the cover of Nicholas Evan's novel *The Horse Whisperer*, and Robert Redford told me he wanted to use the stallion for the film's posters, billboards and print ads.

Thus because of Miguel Ángel Cárdenas, two horses from Écija are undoubtedly the most seen horses in the world. But that was not the end of Vasallo in my books. Again I photographed him, this time for *Stallion of a Dream* and for *Equus Reined*. So esteemed was his image that of the thousands of equines I have photographed, he was used for the logo-type for The Vavra Collection, a stock photo agency, whose clients include Twentieth Century Fox, Disney Studios, Random House, Max Factor, Renault, Roche and Revlon.

Since those times so long ago – I was 43 then, now I'm 69 – I have often visited Miguel Ángel and Carmen in Écija, always anxious to see the new horses at the San Pablo breeding farm or to observe recent additions to their stunning home. One especially memorable visit was when I took Bo Derek to the San Pablo breeding facility. Whose eyes could not be dazzled by the most beautiful of women among the most magnificent of horses – those of Cárdenas. Miguel Ángel's stallions, however, have attracted other Hollywood glamour – including Michael Douglas and Keanu Reeves – to Écija.

During our many years of friendship, though the Cárdenas ranch and home have experienced great change, what remains the same are Miguel Ángel and Carmen, he with his passion for Spanish Horses and breeding the finest animals possible. To Miguel Ángel, horses are not merely part of life, they are his life. And Carmen compliments him with her directness and eye for decoration and her passion for literature – more than 5,000 books line the shelves of her library. With my love of Africa and books, it would seem impossible to find a Spanish Horse breeder's wife, let alone from Écija, with whom I could discuss (in English or Spanish,) Karen Blixen, Leni Riefenstahl, Ernest Hemingway, Sir Wilfred Thesiger, or Beryl Markham. However, Carmen's interest and knowledge is wide and includes gardening and classical music, as well as the worthy causes she champions.

When I am off in the bush in Kenya, Tanzania, Zimbabwe or Botswana, I sometimes think of Miguel Ángel's fascination and knowledge of history and his dry sense of humor. But most of all, I envision the steady gaze of his serene blue eyes fixed on one of the stallions at San Pablo. I see him patting the whiteness of the stallion Mástil, the most expressive horse I have ever photographed. Or I picture him in thought, trying to determine how he can make the photographic settings for his horses more attractive for the dozens and dozens of cameramen who visit San Pablo, including Thomas Kilper, Tomas Miček, Till Leeser, and me, who have enjoyed his enthusiasm and hospitality. Unlimited are his efforts to share the beauty of his stallions with people everywhere.

And far off at my Kenyan campfire, when Carmen comes to mind, I imagine her in the home's upstairs expansive trophy salon, as she is illuminated by a ray of light from a window which also brings brightness to a slight trail of incense smoke rising upward and upward and upward toward the room's lofty ceiling. Or I picture Carmen with her dachshunds Blonde, Caruso, but mostly Maquroll, his head on her lap as she strokes the silkiness of his short, fine, rich brown coat.

In conclusion, the word Cárdenas signifies friends, horses and home. It means 'gente del caballo,' people of the horse, of whom Miguel Ángel and Carmen are two of the equine world's most distinguished members.

The purpose of this book is to share this very special couple and their very special horses and home with all people who love equines and beauty.

Now turn this page to come face to face with Vasallo, Mástil, Clásico, Genil and Ecuador, along with eighty Cárdenas mares. Beyond them you will find the door to the intimate magnificence of the Cárdenas home. Your hosts are Miguel Ángel Cárdenas Osuna and his wife Maria del Carmen Jimenez-Alfaro, Countess of Prado Castellano. Your guide, their devoted friend who writes these words. Come with me and enter their special world…

THE GALLERIES

Nature is more beautiful than art...

Buffon

At the age of ten, with a Kodak Box Camera, I took my first equine image. It was 1945, when the Second World War ended and my subjects were riding stable veterans in a rickety wooden corral on the edge of Steinbeck country – Taft, California. Like the fence lizards watching us, my brother Ron and I spent hours in the blazing sun, hanging onto those grey splintery rails. How we loved what we saw, what we smelled and what we heard – horses.

In 1952, I once more focused a camera on the animals I have loved since memory, as matador turned rejoneador, or bullfighter from horseback, Carlos Arruza galloped around the Tijuana ring on one of his magnificent Iberian stallions.

Later in Spain where, at age twenty-three, I had gone to do a behavioral study of fighting cattle, I would again focus a camera on the magnificence of Spanish Horses. How clearly I recall moments spent with friend and legendary matador Juan Belmonte at his ranch, Gómez Cardeña. Still fresh in my mind is the picture of him on a white Andalusian, a distant speck against the expanse of grey olive trees. That image represents all that is meaningful between horse and man. In those years I was mostly using black and white film for horse images published in *Bulls of Iberia, Curro: Reflections of a Spanish Youth, The Sevilla of Carmen* and *Iberia,* done with James A. Michener.

Then in 1977, came the opportunity to do in color *Equus: the creation of a horse.* Never has my work in books, calendars, etc., appeared with the pictures of other camera artists. Why? Because I felt I could not remain true to the singular style I envisioned if my work was reproduced along side horse pictures of a different perspective.

Interestingly enough, over the years, the best horse photographs I have seen have been done by cameramen like myself, who focus their lenses on a range of subjects, from Maasai warriors to movie stars. None are strictly "horse photographers."

Now for the first time in almost half a century my horse pictures appear here with those of other photographers: Tomas Kepler, Till Leeser and Tomas Miček who apart from stallions, mares and foals, focus on automobiles, fashion models and rain forests. So why break the rule to always stand alone with my equine images? Because the reason for this book is to show the extreme beauty of the Cárdenas horses who have been photographed by dozens of cameramen. And it seemed the best way that beauty could be displayed was not by one man, but several, each with his distinct style.

So, here we have four galleries of pictures of some of the most stunning equines in the world: Vasallo, Clásico, Genil, Ecuador, Mástil, Valido, Vandalo, Ungido, Jubiloso, as they dazzle each man's lens as much as the beauty of Spanish stallions inspired the brushes of Velázquez and Rubens.

The Spanish Horses parading the walls of Prado and other museums were from different breeding farms. Those on the pages of this book are all of the brand of Cárdenas, a testimony to the treasures that are foaled each year at the farm of San Pablo near Écija.

THOMAS KILPER

He was
magnificent.
Deep-chested
and strong in
the quarters...
His coat was
a perfect white.

Nicholas Evans

Sometimes he trots as if told the steps, with gentle majesty and modest pride.

Shakespeare

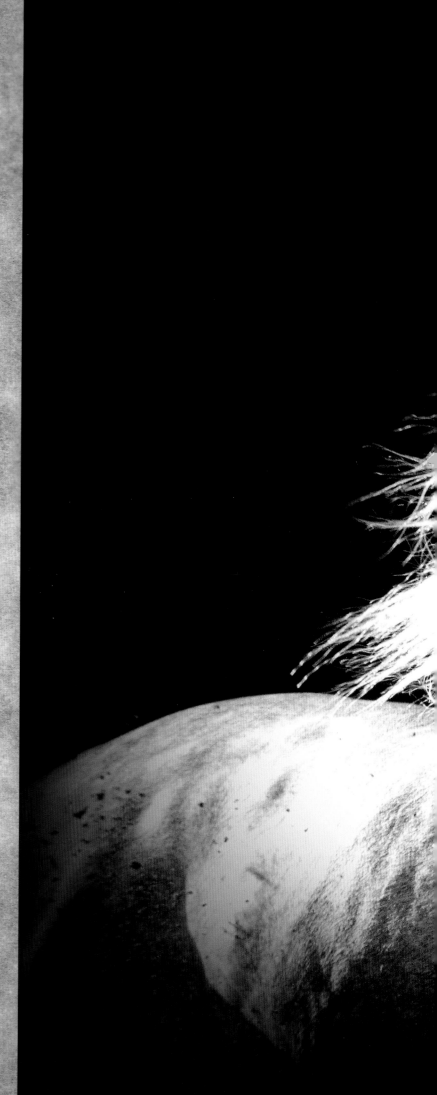

*L*end me the stone strength of the past and I will lend you the wings of the future, for I have them.

Robinson Jeffers

TOMAS MIČEK

The Spanish Horse is the noblest horse in the world, the most beautiful that can be...
the lovingest, gentlest, and the fittest of all for a king on his day of triumph.

The Duke of Newcastle

VASALLO

From the Prado
I now prance,
to Falla's Spanish dance.

Trajan Tennent

...I am fearfully and wonderfully made.

Psalms 139:14

*I*mperiously he leaps,
he neighs, he bounds.

Shakespeare

*He was not of an age
but for all time.*

Ben Jonson

VALIDO
(Lida and Tomas Miček)

Antonio Camborio

would

ride

me

if

he could

Federico

from

Granada

would

have

sung it so.

Trajan Tennent

GENIL
(Lida and Tomas Miček)

*I*t will be long before there
is born, if ever,
an Andalusian so frank,
so rich in adventure.
I sing your elegance
with words that moan
and remember a sad wind
among the olive trees.

Federico García Lorca

*The sight of
that horse did
something to me
I've never been
able to explain.
He was more
than tremendous
strength and speed
and beauty of
motion. He set
me dreaming.*

Walt Morey

...nothing can
bring back the
hour of splendor
in the grass,
of glory in
the flower...

William Wordsworth

Flamenco beat.
Fandango,
farruca,
solear.
Hooves
echoing,
echoing, far.

Trajan Tennent

JUBILOSO
(Lida and Tomas Miček)

*Look, what a horse
should have
he did not lack,
Save a proud rider
on his back.*

Shakespeare

VASALLO
(Lida and Tomas Miček)

48

*U*nder the smooth satin skin, the muscles rolled and played... His legs were straight, clean,... He was temperamental... He was proud... He was an aristocrat...

Joseph Tenebaum

VASALLO
(Lida and Tomas Miček)

This is the attitude used
by artists to depict the
horses on which gods and
heroes ride...

Xenophon

TILL LEESER

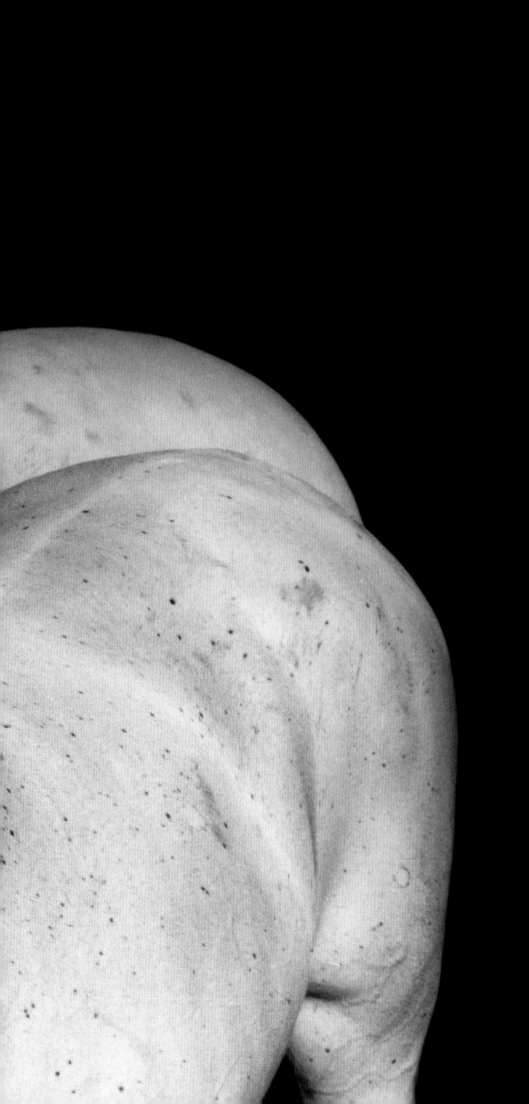

*L*ead me to *E*ija's mares' white flanks and angel hair.

Trajan Tennent

The horse is a creature who sacrifices his being to exist through the will of another... he is the noblest conquest of man.

Buffon

UNGIDO
ROYAL STABLES, CORDOBA

(Over page)

...a horse is a beautiful animal, but it is perhaps most remarkable because it moves as if it always hears music.

Marc Helprin

UNGIDO

...in the whiteness of the
white, flowering in the
tattered water, their bodies
arching with streaked
marble... riding in like...
silver ships.

Peter S. Beagle

The hooves of the horse!
Oh! Witching and sweet
is the music earth steals
from the iron-shod feet;
No whisper of love,
no trilling of bird,
can stir me as
hooves of the horse
have stirred.

Will H. Ogilvie

Necks arched, ears alert...
Grey their layers of silky
coats,
Swift their agile, eager legs;
gracefully running...
To the plain of Écija town.

Fernando Villalón

*God forbid that
I should go to
any heaven in
which there are
no horses.*

R. B. Cunningham-Graham

$\mathcal{T}$he earth sings when
he touches it;
the basest horn of his
hooves is more musical
than the pipes of Hermes...

Shakespeare

H is soaring pivot
Ushered heaven to earth
In a plummet of hooves.

Michael Masley

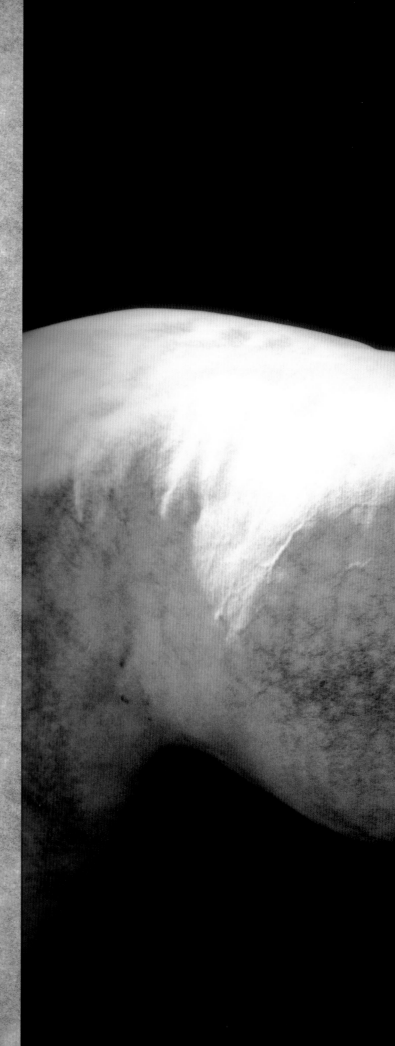

He was what every
horse wanted to be...
hooves of silver,
a mane soft and thick
as a waving cloud,
a neck strong as a
Roman arch...
and a broad back
smooth as lakewater...

Louis Untermeyer

ROBERT VAVRA

Images of Vasallo from the documentary *Such is the Real Nature of Horses*

He is swift and strong among the swift ones, but it is that flowing mane and tail that mark him chiefly from afar.

Ernest Thompson Seton

VASALLO

...we stretched up into the air,
fleeting on in the sunshine
A speck in the gleam
On galloping hoofs, his mane
in the wind out-flowing
As if in a dream...

Walter de la Mare

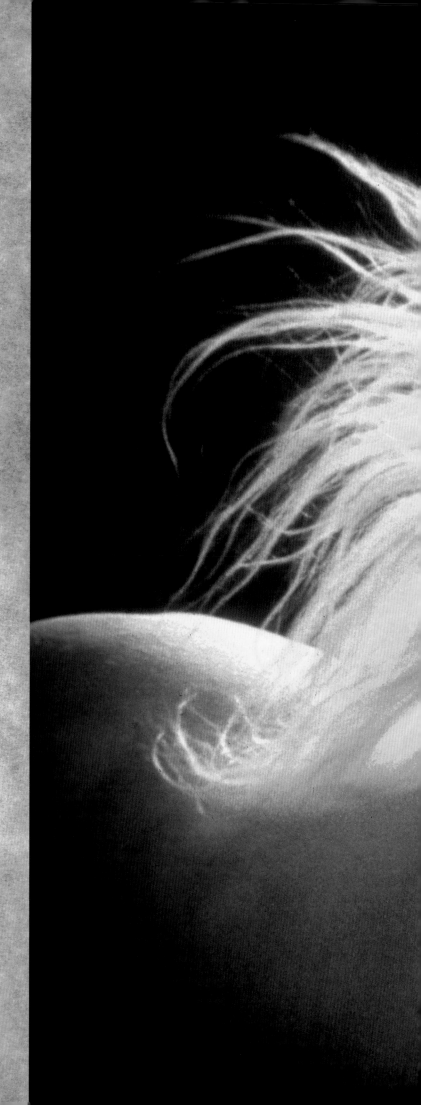

Pegasus was a snow white steed... as wild, and as swift, and as buoyant, in his flight through the air, as any eagle that ever soared into the clouds.

Nathaniel Hawthorne

$\mathcal{M}$y hand forever in
your mane so dense,
Rubies and pearls and
sapphires there will sow...
Oasis of my dreams,
and gourd from whence
Deep drafted wines of
memory will flow.

Charles Baudelaire

VASALLO

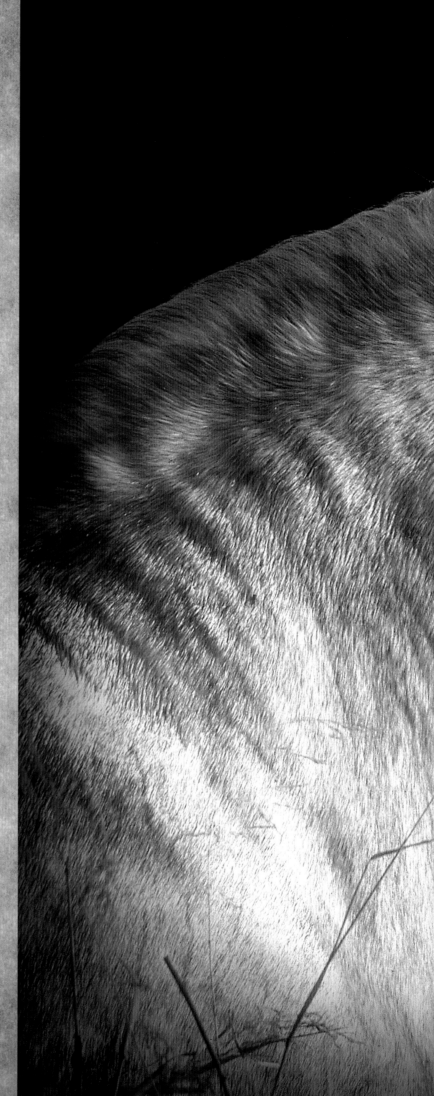

Of all animals kept for the recreation of mankind, the horse is alone capable of exciting a passion that is absolutely hopeless.

Bret Harte

From near the city of Cordoba comes our Cardenas name. Moorish mosque and Manolete's fame.

Trajan Tennent

Who shod the flying thunders on their feet... And plumed them with the

snortings of the sea... Surely the great white breakers gave them birth.
Roy Campbell

Like waves that follow o're the sea ...horses Came thickly thundering on.

Lord Byron

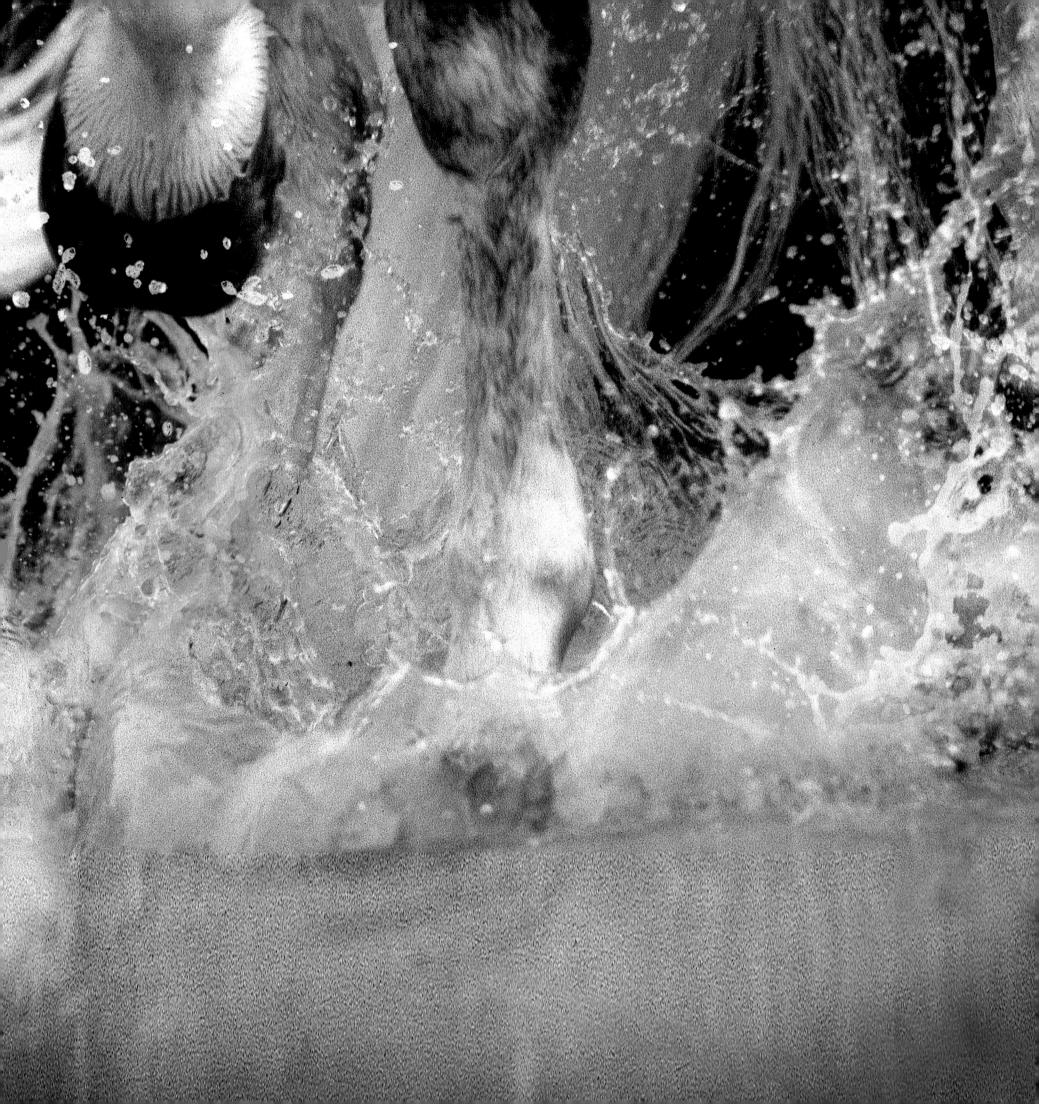

How nervous and keen
he was with his small
head and his fine legs!

Juan Ramón Jiménez

I have immortal longings.

Shakespeare

*I*nventing a story
with grass I find
a young horse deep
inside it.

James Dickey

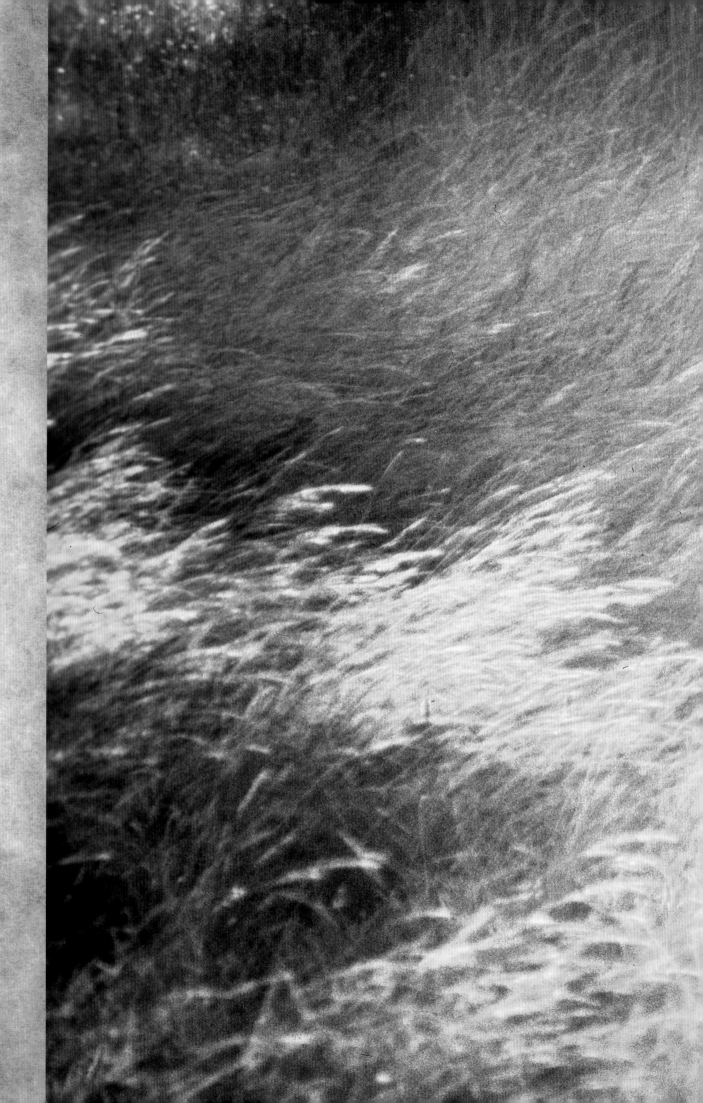

...presently he would wheel around and stare in another direction, pointing his ears forward to listen to some faint far sound which had touched his senses.

William Henry Hudson

$\mathcal{T}$he back of thy horse subjects the world to thee. I will fashion it into a throne for thee; whence thou shalt yield a sceptre of power and joy and freedom, such as is beyond expectation.

Rudolph C. Binding

$\mathcal{B}$ucephalus
would have
envied
me.
Alexander
ridden
me.
Velázquez
painted me.

Trajan Tennent

...he is pure air and fire; and the dull elements of earth and water never appear in him...
He looks upon his love, and neighs unto her...

Shakespeare

ECUADOR

(Over page)

What a joy.
To sit on his back
like a throne,
to touch heaven
while still on earth,
remain together for
many years,
companions in journeys
and dreams!

Juan Llamas

MÁSTIL, SPANISH WALK; GITANO, PIAFFE;
CLÁSICO, PASSAGE; FUEGO, EXTENDED TROT

$\mathcal{W}$here in this world can
man find nobility
without pride, friendship
without envy, beauty
without vanity?
  Here, where grace is
laced with muscle and
strength by gentleness
confined……

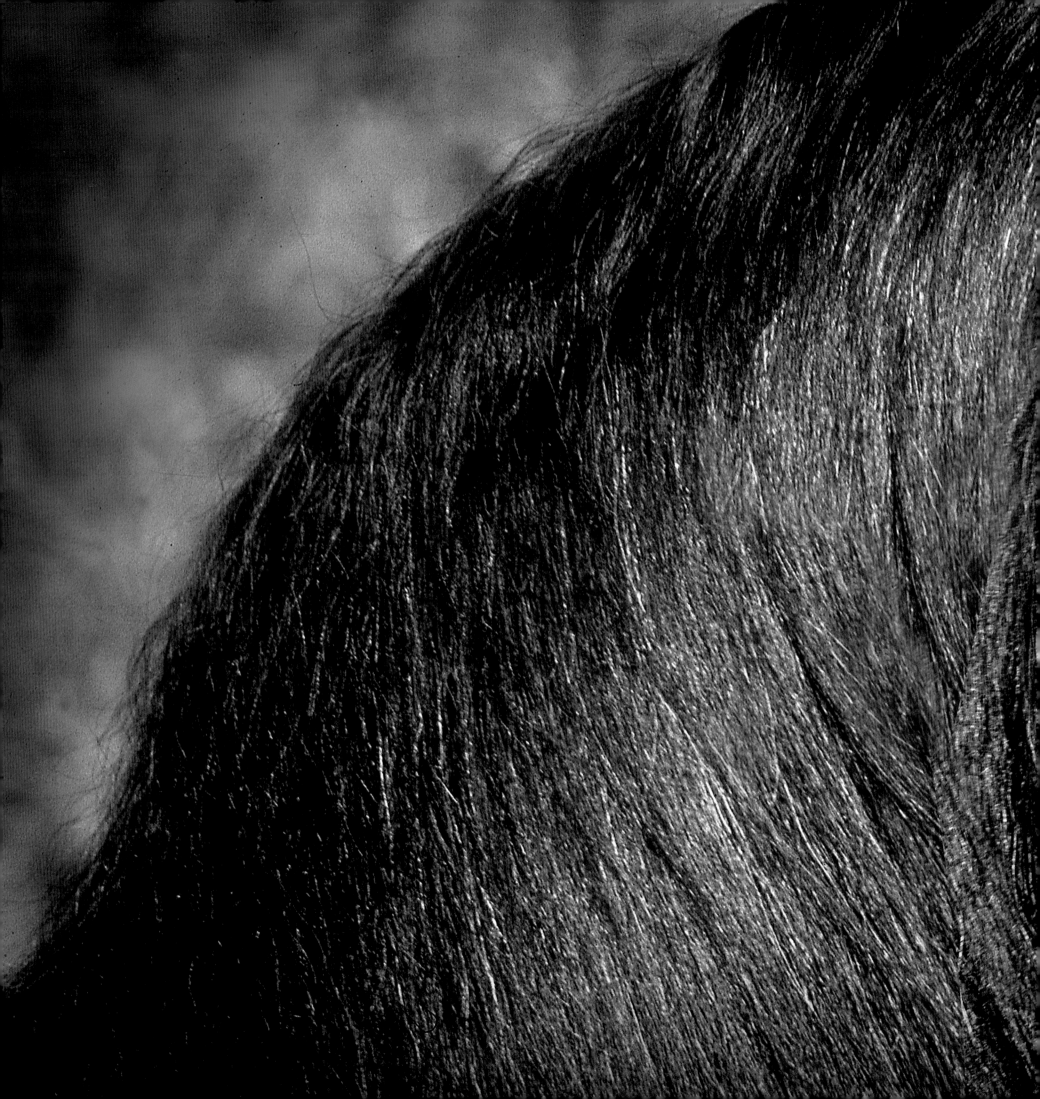

He serves without servility;
he fought without enmity.
There is nothing so powerful,
nothing less violent; there is
nothing so quick, nothing more
patient...

Robert Duncan

124

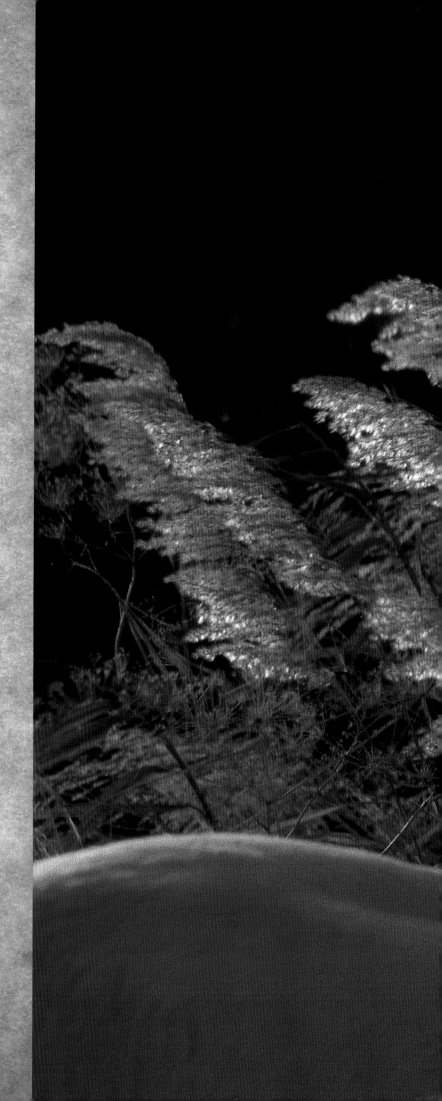

There was a
light breeze
that
played through
the stallion's
forelock
and
mane...
bringing with
it scents of
orange blossoms
of Seville,
sherry
of Jerez,
jasmine
of Granada,
tuber roses
of Cordoba,
and salt
of Cadiz.

Trajan Tennent

The wind is a horse;
hear how he runs...
through the sky.
...listen how he roves
the world...

Pablo Neruda

FUEGO

(Over page)

Pure and disposed to
mount into the stars.

Dante

The flashing cascade of his mane, the curving comet of his tail, invested him with housings more resplendent than gold and silver bearers could have furnished him.

Herman Melville

CLÁSICO

(Over page) GENIL

*G*reatness knows itself.

Shakespeare

CLÁSICO

(Over page)

*O*h! *M*ares of *É cíja*
so nobly accepting the
will of man,
While in sisterhood
your true nature does
command.

Trajan Tennent

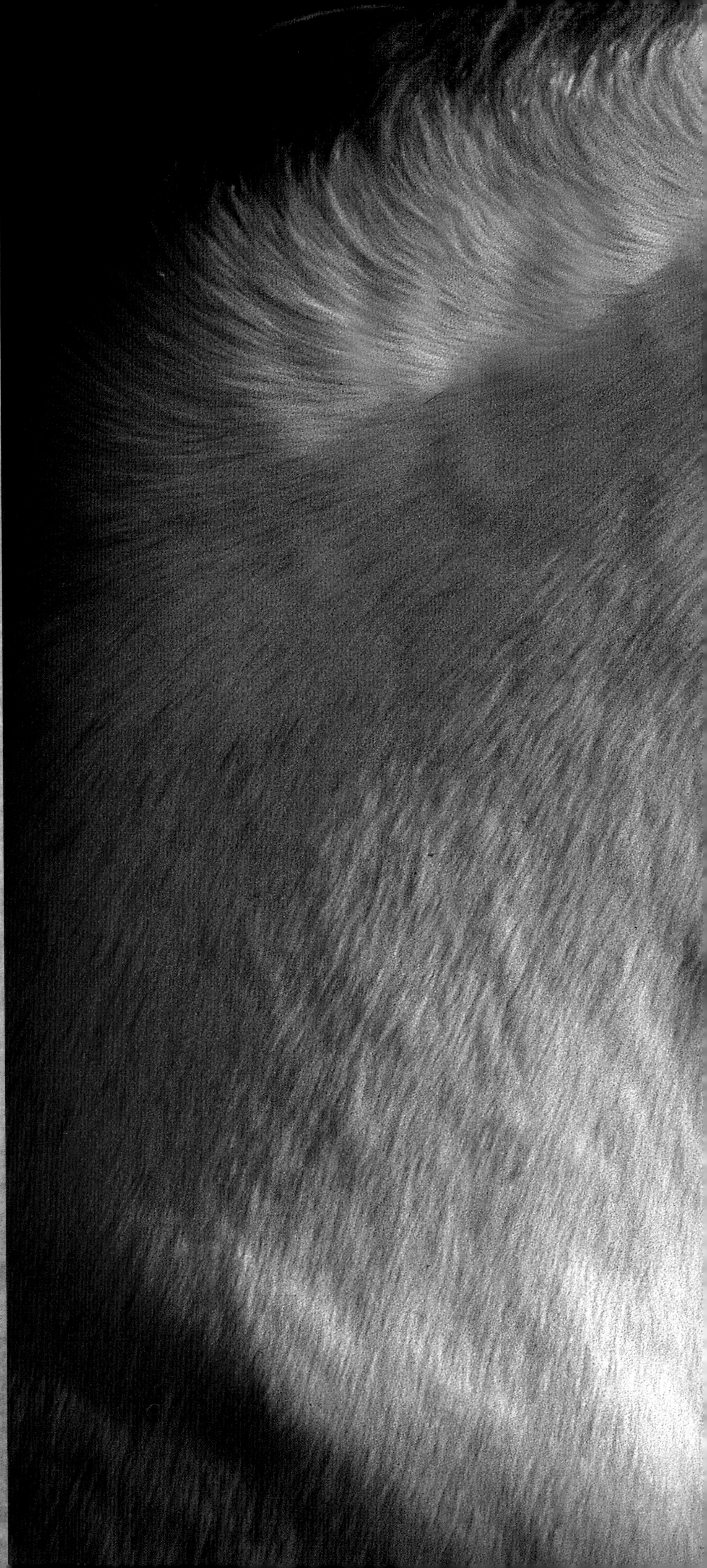

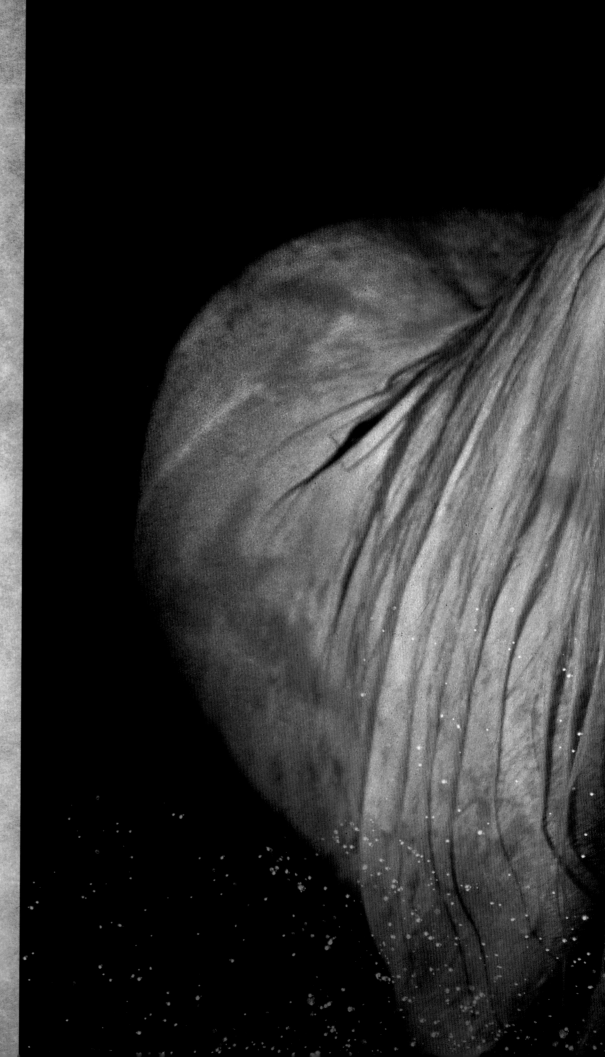

I must go down
to the sea again,
For the call of the
running tide
Is a wild call
and a clear call
That may not be
denied.

John Masefield

VANDALO

(Over page) MÁSTIL

$\mathcal{T}$he stallion was
surging on...
his eyes open
against the spray...
A wall of steel
flesh broadside to
the wave...

Charles Tenny Jackson

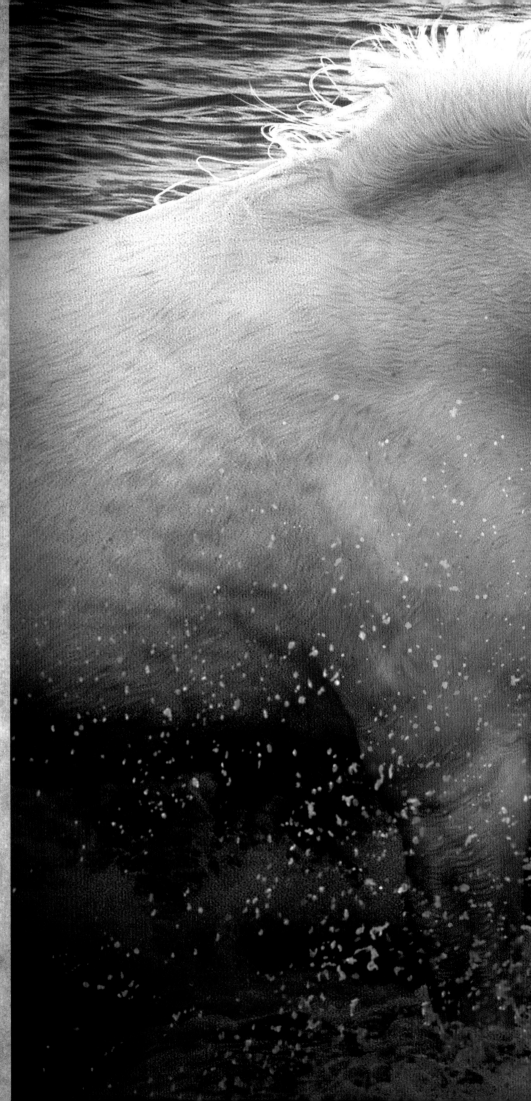

$\mathcal{N}$ow the wild white horses play.
Champ and chafe and toss in
the spray.

Matthew Arnold

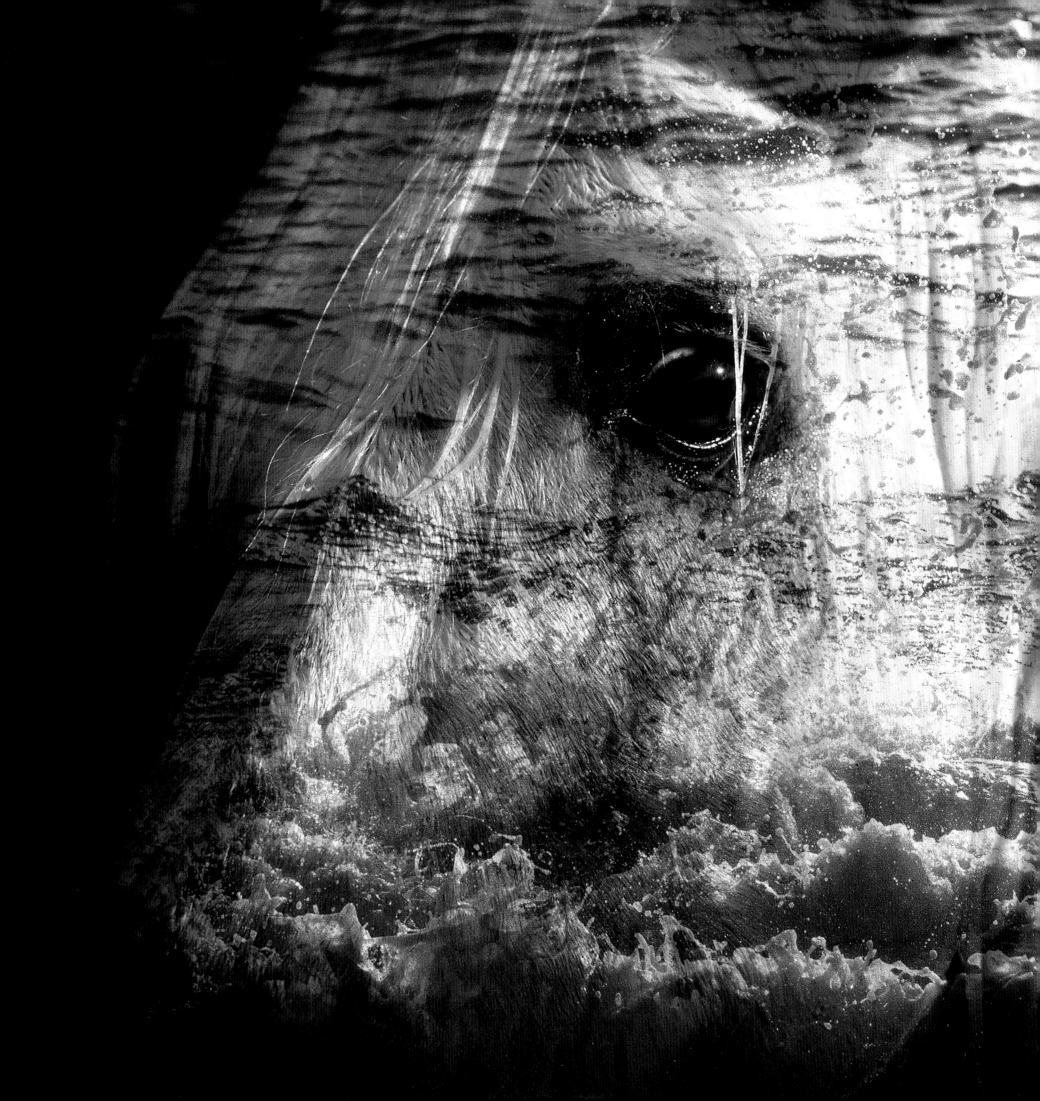

...stampeding horse,
that raves...
when it
meets the sea at last
is swallowed outright
by the waves.

Federico García Lorca

We know that when the horse negotiated the land bridge... he found on the other end an opportunity for varied development that is one of the bright aspects of animal history... He would journey into Spain where his very name would become the designation of a gentleman, a caballero, a man of the horse. There he would flourish mightily and serve the armies that would conquer much of the known world.

James A. Michener

The ranch of San Pablo is on the outskirts of Écija — the Cárdenas house is in the center of a city of 38,000 people. From the air, the estate appears like a lush green gardened, tile-roofed architectural dream surrounded by Lorca's "white wall(s) of Spain." Écija does have some grand houses, but the Cárdenas grounds and home are unparalleled.

In the tradition of Arab cities in which palatial homes are often hidden among the humble abodes of the populace, Miguel Ángel and Carmen's home is barely visible to the casual pedestrian. After walking by a pharmacy, hardware store and modest, white-washed houses, one would have to glance by chance to the right from Carreras Street and down narrow Santa Florentina Street to encounter the magnificent façade of the Cárdenas home.

From Seville Street, however, can be seen the restored Moorish tower beneath which (hidden from the street) the eye is dazzled by other recently re-created treasures from the past: arches, an expansive stone fountain – the stone floor is a work of art by itself – all crafted by the most skilled of artisans.

Upon entering Miguel Ángel and Carmen's home, one is as much aware of Carmen's superior gift for decorative beauty and design as the San Pablo mares and stallions reveal her husband's eye for equine beauty and the creation of it.

Now it is time to visit the Cárdenas home. And after the reader has wandered its gardens and marveled at the magnificence of its salons, Carmen, at the end of this "short tour," describes the history of all that lies beyond the door you are about to enter. Excerpts from this text appear with the photographs that follow.

WAYNE CHASAN

Art Direction by Robert Vavra

The house we live in must have been built in the mid-XVIth century. The first documents I have seen say that D. Gregorio de Guzmán bequeathed the house and his property, next to the Santa Florentina Wall, to his children, Don Diego and Doña Catalina. His daughter Doña Catalina was married to Don Cristóbal Morales y Cárdenas. This couple wrote their will on September 8, 1590. The document refers to the house as an "estate building used as a family dwelling." Since the daughter wrote her will in 1590, consequently her father must have signed his last will at least twenty-five years beforehand. Therefore, it is possible to calculate that the house was built around the middle of the XVIth century.

HOME'S XVIII CENTURY FACADE

$\mathcal{T}$he house was built on a corner of the Ronda road, the fortress walkway of the city, leading to the Muwahhadi (Moorish) Tower, the ancient gate to Seville. Later on, during the XVIIIth century the walls were neglected. They were used to add other buildings under which they remained partly hidden, resulting in an alignment with the new inner-city layout.

The census registry of the Parrish of Collación de Santa Cruz in 1693 refers to Don Rodrigo de Morales y Cárdenas who lived in the house. He was the brother of Don Antonio, First Marquis of Garantia in Naples. Both are owners of the estate.

During the following years, the estate was used as the residential home of the families Guzmán y Zayas and Morales Cárdenas.

(Over page) STALLIONS IN COURTYARD: JUNCO, MÁSTIL, VANDALO, CLÁSICO

In 1704, the estate passed to another member of the family, Don Rodrigo Morales Cárdenas.

My father-in-law, Miguel Ángel de Cárdenas Lavanera, bought the estate on December 29, 1970, from the heirs of the last Marquis, for his son Miguel Ángel de Cárdenas Osuna,

my husband. Thus, after almost three hundred years, the surname Cárdenas returned to the estate, a family that had once lived in it for several generations and had formerly owned the property.

GREEK ALABASTER HORSE HEAD

Finally, on the 2nd of April 1970, (Saint Francis of Paula's day) we slept in the house for the first time. We chose that day, because it was my father's saint's day, who had passed away a year before.

I had spent my childhood in an old declining garden full of trees where the sun scarcely entered and the type of vegetation was limited, but which had, and still has, its own special charm. Now I felt I had to do something different with Miguel Ángel's and my new home. Soon I began creating a garden with consecutive planes on different levels, flowered walls, variation of color, with streams, orange and cypress trees, and jasmine... a continuation of patios leading to one another: Córdoba, Granada, Roman Andalusia... pure Mediterranean...

So is the garden of my dreams, the one I long and search for, in which I do my gardening and with increased anticipation plan for every new season.

Fernando Villalón wrote:

The paths of the garden
draw their own lines:
my feet write your letters
with unnoticed designs.

GARDEN

(Over page) MÁSTIL IN THE GARDEN

BOUGAINVILLEA IN THE PATIO OF THE FRAGRANCIES

I remember the first time that the garden burst with color and I picked up a blossom which seemed a welcoming gesture, making me definitively feel at home.

Later, in 1985, we again started on the renovation, extending the garden at the end of the farm house where there were some abandoned workrooms; on the upper level we built a swimming pool "Natatio" with the appearance of a pond, surrounded by three landscaped patios...

Walking the garden path, in early morning or late afternoon, I recall a poem by Beatriz Cort:

Iron gates that open and close,
Beauty and mystery, rich vegetation
Only seen in dreams.
The soul of the plant embraces us
With arms blue, red, green.

We attempted to keep the original layout of the house, characteristic of this city, following this rule throughout in regard to proportion of spaces, building materials, including type of wood, as well as bricks manufactured here in the same way the Romans use to make them. Called 'Ecijan brick' by architects and contractors, they are sought for construction throughout Andalusia.

MAIN STAIRWAY

LADY OF THE HOUSE OF ORANGE
17TH CENTURY

*I*n the main drawing room downstairs, *Miguel Ángel,* who has a passion for history, has a splendid collection of horse books.

When I was young, books played a major role in my parents' house. All of us, my mother, my father, my brother and I had our books that grew in number every year. Today I almost have 5,000 volumes starting from those first ones that I began to gather as a girl... What books do we have? History, art, literature, biographies, chosen and searched for according to the moments of my life.

I value a rare edition book, but I am not a bibliophile. I love books, not for their economic value, but for what they have to say, what is written in them, for the author and for what he describes.

DETAIL FROM A PAINTING ON COPPER

Miguel Ángel has bought the finest paintings and tapestries. He chooses the best, always with a clear good taste for making the right choice. He possesses the gift of magnificence, a rare and special trait, according to one of our very dearest friends, the late Father Antonio García del Moral... Most of the furniture has been left to us by our parents; I believe they are good quality, as well as beautiful pieces and, therefore, worth keeping both for their value and their provenance.

GUEST BATHROOM WINDOW

$\mathcal{W}$e enjoy entertaining and having guests, friends, family...

GUEST ROOM

MAQUROLL IN DINING ROOM

An indescribable being that still doesn't know if he is a dog, a person or a goblin, goes by the name of Maquroll El Gaviero, in homage and memory of the main character of the author Álvaro Muttis, the Colombian writer who I so admire.

I have always had a feeling for fantasy, like being suspended between the real and the unreal. This fantasy with as much spirituality as possible, helps so much and enlightens the things that give us comfort in the home. I place or move objects for something more profound than what they are, because they grant me peace.

UPSTAIRS HALLWAY

I do not have a predetermined style for interior decoration. I simply like to be surrounded by the things that I'm fond of, that are a part of my life or that bring me memories of somebody or something, a voyage souvenir. A gift from a loved one or from someone who knows us well. Things that put color into our life...

I like crystal (uncolored), antique silver, and also modern silver if it is a piece of art and Spanish ceramic. Boxes, I love boxes. Not the little ones. I don't like repetition and collections bore me.

Every night I walk through the rooms and put the house to sleep, first the dogs and then, I give a look throughout the home and symbolically "I tuck her into bed." I like doing this very much.

I love to have candles glowing, mainly those made of natural wax. "Because God loves the light of the lamps of man, more than the big stars of the heavens."

(Over page)
LANDAU IN COURTYARD

R*emembering* L*uis* C*ernuda:*

Away in the garden
seated by the fountain
dreaming about life
with endless delight.

CARMEN WITH "GNOMES"

I am not very sure whether or not we have ghosts. I imagine we do. But I am perfectly sure gnomes live among us, little goblins; they are my dachshunds, amusing, humbugs; going in and out from one place to another without stopping, as a living example of perpetual motion.

I do not like to use the word decoration for my own house, arranging the home is not decorating it, it is living in it, it is feeling at home, warmed by the soul of the inanimated objects that speak about themselves: what they are, what they were, why they are here.

UPSTAIRS GALLERY WITH DOORWAY TO TROPHY ROOM
PORTRAIT OF MÁSTIL BY MARIANO AGUAYO

All of our friends fill our home with pleasant memories, including painter Mariano Aguayo and his wife Fernanda. Mariano's magnificent portrait of the stallion Mástil not only decorates the stairway to the trophy room, but gives the horse a permanent presence in our home.

On the way to the library and next to it is the main living room, where we keep all the stud trophies, memorabilia, photos... pictures of the effort and determination of an entire life, of my husband's passion for the Spanish Horse and the Cárdenas lineage.

I adore burning incense and lavender mixed with myrrh and bergamot, "Sacreligious Perfume" as my mother used to call it. It is an old family recipe, with a scent, both a warm and fresh.

VIEW OF MOORISH TOWER FROM TROPHY SALON

The library is on the first floor, in what was an old hay barn above the XVIIIth century stable. We transformed it almost fifteen years ago, and since then I continue to place all my books in the bookcases that Pepe the carpenter has built for me.

The extension of the estate continues, partly due to the project of the Cordoban architect, Arturo Ramírez, supporting Miguel Ángel's desire (another display of magnificence) to embellish this part of the city, demolishing a series of little houses, bought over the last years, that were built on the remains of the fortress wall that has now been reinstated.

GENIL, JUNCO, ECUADOR AND SOME OF THE MORE THAN ONE HUNDRED AND TWENTY CÁRDENAS MARES IN THE PATIO OF THE ROSE FOUNTAIN

ECUADOR

Today, with the further expansion at the front of the estate, we have an entrance patio at the foot of the Moorish tower with two tall cypresses and African lilies, a magnolia tree, trumpet vine climbers and Santa Catalina's trough.

COBRA OF MARES IN FRONT
OF THE MOORISH TOWER

(Over page)

Next to it there is a great central patio with a fountain surrounded by four palm trees with creeping rosemary around them. Turkish lemon trellis and bougainvillea climb the fortress wall and several trees stand next to the Loggia gallery in front of the central fountain.

COBRA OF MARES IN THE PATIO OF THE ROSE
FOUNTAIN IN FRONT OF THE HOME'S FACADE

$\mathcal{H}$ouses remain longer than do we... we disappear soon. We put into them, especially in this case, so much energy and so many illusions, so many feelings... Good moments and not so good, hoping that a part of us will remain among the trees and in the ripple of the fountain, so whoever may wander by may listen to the silence and perhaps feel the warmth of our heart that was left here while we lived.

To conclude, I remember Saint Jerome's words of the second century in his XIIth epistle to the Galations:

...We live as if we shall die tomorrow, and we build as if we shall live forever.

MIGUEL ÁNGEL CÁRDENAS

"...to breed a noble horse is to share with God one of His mysteries. As well as one of His delights."

HISTORY OF THE HOME
REFLECTIONS
PHOTO ALBUM
EPILOGUE
ACKNOWLEDGEMENTS

THE HOME: PAST AND PRESENT

La Condesa de Prado Castellano

Écija is located next to the river Genil, between Córdoba and Seville, on the edge of the latter province. Originally named ASTIGI, it was founded by Astur, the Greek.

During the Roman occupation, Écija flourished into great splendor as Colony Augusta Firma, being the capital of one of the administrative jurisdictions of The Bética. The city contains countless and priceless works of art of that period and the subsoil is an endless source of hidden, valuable artifacts of exceptional beauty and quality.

Later, the Visigoths turned Écija into an outstanding cultural and religious society.

During the Muslim occupation of Spain, the primitive name of Estigga was again used for the city, although it was also known as Medina Al' Coton (the city of the cotton) because of its great agricultural production.

The King of Castile, Fernando III The Holy, won back the town in 1240 and his son, Alfonso X The Wise, distributed the land among the conquerors. In 1404, Enrique III granted the title of "City" to Écija, and in 1770 Felipe V proclaimed it "Constant, Loyal and very Faithful."

The XVIIIth century was considered the golden age of Écija. Fertile land and the power of its many resident noble families were in perfect balance with the cultural and the religious influence of the clergy. These two sectors of the society blended with a third factor just as important as the previous ones, which were the many guilds of artisans and merchants (more than 24) that had considerable diversity and great significance and authority.

As a result of these positive factors, the city was modernized. All over, private construction began, as well as the repair of churches, most of which had been severely damaged by the recent Lisbon earthquake. Houses and palaces were also renovated and embellished turning Écija into the baroque jewel that it is today.

In the XIXth century, the city fell into decline, all members of religious orders were expelled, and many convents were totally abandoned. The churches were also vandalized and the whole city suffered hardship. The increased absence of families, which were once linked historically to the city, began to take effect, pushing many landowners and businessmen into bankruptcy and causing the overall economy to plunge.

In 1996, the city was acknowledged as being of artistic and historical interest. At present, in the beginning of this new millennium, Écija has awakened and is widely regaining its past splendor.

I have been able to compile the previous facts and the following information from the municipal and parish archives where they are meticulously filed.

The house we live in must have been built in the

mid-XVIth century. The first documents I have seen say that D. Gregorio de Guzmán bequeathed the house and his property, next to the Santa Florentina Wall, to his children, Don Diego and Doña Catalina. His daughter Doña Catalina was married to Don Cristóbal Morales y Cárdenas. This couple wrote their will on September 8, 1590. The document refers to the house as an "estate building used as a family dwelling." Since the daughter wrote her will in 1590, consequently her father must have signed his last will at least twenty-five years before. Therefore, it is possible to calculate that the house was built around the middle of the XVIth century.

What was the layout of the buildings at the time? The front gallery, as it is today, already existed. This was adjacent to the large hall where presently our equine awards and trophies are kept. Also, a few other outbuildings were clustered around the entry patio (the stable was added in the XVIIIth century) including the farmhouse and the agricultural facilities.

The house was built on a corner of the Ronda road, the fortress walkway of the city, leading to the Muwahhadi (Moorish) Tower, the ancient gate to Seville. Later on, during the XVIIIth century the walls were neglected. They were used to add other buildings under which they remained partly hidden, resulting in an alignment with the new inner-city layout.

The census registry of the Parish of Collación de Santa Cruz in 1693 refers to Don Rodrigo de Morales y Cárdenas who lived in the house. He was the brother of Don Antonio, First Marquis of Garantía in Naples. Both were owners of the estate.

During the following years, the estate was used as the residential home of the families Guzmán and Zayas and Morales Cárdenas.

In 1704, the estate passed to another member of the family, Don Rodrigo Morales Cárdenas and was occupied by his butler Don Antonio Guevara. This situation was repeated from then onward since the gentlemen belonging to the Royal Militia were always absent and their servants maintained their homes.

In 1781, there were no more descendants of the Marquis of Garantía and the estate become the property of the Martel family. They improved the house with a late baroque, near neoclassic facade, placing their coat of arms above the large, wooden front doors of the entryway.

In 1816, the Martel family was able to prove their relationship to the former owner and acquired his title. This was accomplished with the necessary witnesses and documents that establish their relationship with the original holders of the deed. (I have found all this information in the public archives of the Land Registry Office.)

My father-in-law, Miguel Ángel de Cárdenas Llavanera, bought the estate on December 29, 1970, from the heirs of the last Marquis, for his son Miguel Ángel de Cárdenas Osuna, my husband. Thus, after almost three hundred years, the surname Cárdenas returned to the estate, a family that had once lived in it for several generations and had formerly owned the property.

When my father-in-law acquired the estate, the buildings were in very bad shape. In the main building, the great halls had been turned into storage barns and the main arrival patio was overgrown with weeds. The main stairway was a ramshackle, and the interior patio that should be of XVIIIth century style had been renovated in 1897 with modernistic columns. The original columns of the old patio were discovered at the farm house and are now placed as ornamental elements of the garden. There were also abandoned outbuildings, barns, and so on, along with three other houses that had been added toward the end of the XIXth century and beginning of the XXth.

* * * * * * * * * *

What did we do with this abandoned house that was in ruins?

With the essential support and the enormous generosity of my father and mother-in-law and under the supervision of architect and great friend Daniel Sánchez Puch, we began a restoration that became almost a total reconstruction of the estate.

The main arrival patio was enlarged. On the left side another gallery was built on top of the already existing one. The ground floor was raised so as to leave an air chamber to avoid dampness (although the height of the ceilings was reduced).

Finally, the 2nd of April 1970 (Saint Francis of Paula's day), we slept in the house for the first time. We chose that day, because it was the saint's day of my father, who had passed away a year before.

Since it was at the beginning of spring, I could finally begin to design and plant the garden. Since I didn't know where to begin, I sought Miguel Ángel's mother's advice. She was an intelligent and beautiful woman and also a very proficient gardener. We had endless conversations, and it was thanks to her that I entered into the wonderful botanical world.

I had spent my childhood in an old declining garden full of trees where the sun scarcely entered and the type of vegetation was limited, but which had, and still has, its own special charm. Now I felt I had to do something different with Miguel Ángel's and my new home. Soon I began creating a garden with consecutive planes on different levels, flowered walls, variations of color, with streams, orange and cypress trees, and jasmine… a continuation of patios leading to one another: Córdoba, Granada, Roman Andalusia… pure Mediterranean.

So is the garden of my dreams, the one I long and search for, in which I do my gardening and plan for every new season.

The climate here is extreme with a torrid summer and some devastating days of winter, but I believe that every gardening failure guides me toward a new discovery prompted by something I may have seen somewhere or that somebody might have told me about and I want to try.

I remember the first time that the jacaranda tree bloomed. I found a blossom, picked it up, and it seemed like a welcoming gesture, making me definitely feel at home.

Later, in 1985, we again started on the renovation, extending the garden at the end of the farm house where there were some abandoned workrooms; on the upper level we built a swimming pool, "Natatio" with the appearance of a pond, and three landscaped patios: The San Miguel Patio with a large expanse of hand-painted ceramic tile of the archangel over the drinking trough, The Scented Patio, lavender, jasmine, myrtle and rosemary, and another patio at a medium level with clipped cypresses, two orange trees and an Arab fountain in the center.

Today, with the further expansion at the front of the estate, we have an entrance patio at the foot of the Moorish tower with two tall cypresses and African lilies, a magnolia tree, trumpet vine climbers and Santa Catalina's trough.

Next to it there is a great central patio with a fountain surrounded by four palm trees with creeping rosemary around them. Turkish lemon trellis and bougainvillea climb the fortress wall and several trees stand next to the Loggia gallery in front of the central fountain.

I also have in mind a secret garden behind the fortress wall and the tower… a secret garden for my dreams to wander, with a water trough, ferns, seclusion, intimacy, ever-increasing greenery, and shade…

Remembering Luis Cernuda:

> Away in the garden
> seated by the fountain
> dreaming about life
> with endless delight.

✳ ✳ ✳ ✳ ✳ ✳ ✳ ✳ ✳

THE HOUSE

We attempted to keep the original layout of the house, characteristic of this city, following this rule throughout in regard to proportion of spaces, building materials, including type of wood, as well as bricks manufactured here in the same way the Romans used to make them. Called "Écijan brick" by architects and contractors, they are sought for construction throughout Andalusia.

I do not have a predetermined style for interior decoration. I simply like to be surrounded by the things that I'm fond of, that are a part of my life, or that bring me memories of somebody or something. A voyage souvenir. A gift from a loved one or from someone who knows us well. Things that put color into our life and that I also consider beautiful.

I do not like to use the word decoration for my own house. Arranging the home is not decorating it, it is living in it, it is feeling at home, warmed by the soul of the inanimate objects that speak about themselves: what they are, what they were, why they are here. It is also searching for aesthetic appeal so that everything fits together, moving objects around till they find their place, and changing them around yet again when I find the need for it. When I travel, after I have spent some days away from the house, on the evening of my return I change something. I can't help doing so; it is gratifying.

I like crystal (uncolored), antique silver, and also modern silver, if it is a piece of art, and Spanish ceramic. Boxes, I love boxes. Not the little ones. I don't like repetition and collections bore me.

I value a rare edition book, but I am not a bibliophile. I love books, not for their economic value, but for what they have to say, what is written in them, for the author and for what he describes.

I love to have candles glowing, mainly those made of natural wax. "Because God loves the light of the lamps of man, more than the big stars of the heavens."

I adore burning incense and lavender mixed with

myrrh and bergamot, "Sacrilegious Perfume" as my mother used to call it. It is an old family recipe, with both a warm and fresh scent.

I enjoy placing flowers in the house, I choose them from the garden, I pick them and arrange them in vases; it is an entire ceremony. They last a short time, but arranging and admiring them is a vital and a beautiful experience.

I have always had a feeling for fantasy, like being suspended between the real and the unreal. This fantasy, with as much spirituality as possible, helps so much and enlightens the things that give us comfort in the home. I place or move objects for something more profound than what they are, because they grant me peace.

Rosaries give me peace, and also strength; I have them all over the house, on the table, on the windowsill, on a book, on the headrest of a bed, and so on. I touch them when I come across them, hold them in my hand for a while. For me, it is like a kind of prayer.

When Christmas gets closer, particularly after December 8th, I begin to place the nativities, evoking and preparing for Jesus' birth.

Each of them has a special meaning, not only for what they represent but because they are a gift from somebody we especially appreciate.

The Neapolitan nativity, jewel of the XVIIIth century, takes its place in the living room. It is a gift from my very dear friend Maria (Nini) Duchess of Frias, who always gave me her unconditional support; her affection and her exemplary way of being will always be with me. The nativity from Granada I display inside a chest cabinet. Another one, also from the XVIIIth century, that

lost some of the figures but have been replaced by an artisan from Granada, I put in the main stairway niche. One from Bethlehem, carved in olive wood, was brought by my dear cousin Pilar, and I place it on the landing by the main entrance steps. In the first floor gallery goes the one from Chiapas (Mexico), a present from our charming young Mexican friend Marta Jiménez. The one from Nepal is placed in the corridor of the entrance to the large living room; in the library is the one from the Philippines; a popular one is in the kitchen, another of ebony from the Ivory Coast, and so on.

When Christmas is over, I put them all away, praying that I may place them again the following year.

* * * * * * * * *

Most of the furniture has been left to us by our parents; I believe the pieces are good quality, as well as beautiful and, therefore, worth keeping both for their value and their provenance.

Miguel Ángel has bought the finest paintings and tapestries. He chooses the best, always with a clear good taste for making the right choice. He possesses the gift of magnificence, a rare and special trait, according to one of our very dearest friends, the late Father Antonio García del Moral.

When I was young, books played a major role in my parents' house. All of us, my mother, my father, my brother, and I had our books that grew in number every year. Today I have almost 5,000 volumes starting from those first ones that I began to gather as a girl.

What books do we have? History, art, literature, biographies, chosen and searched for according to the moments of my life. Now I continue buying history, biographies, histories of cities, doctoral theses, a lot of French literature and, above all, anything that has to do with Spanish America; I am crazy about their writers, they entertain me, and I like to read them. I look for them with limitless interest and as a reference of our common culture.

Downstairs, in the main living room, Miguel Ángel, who has a passion for history, has a splendid collection of horse books.

The library is on the first floor, in what was an old hay barn above the XVIIIth century stable. We transformed it almost fifteen years ago, and since then I continue to place all my books in the bookcases that Pepe the carpenter has built for me.

The view from the library window is of the XIth century Moorish Tower, recently restored by Miguel Ángel in one of his thrusts of magnificence. Among the bookshelves there is a secluded door through which I can go out to the upper walkway of the fortress wall. This has been reconstructed on its primitive foundations, and leads straight to the tower and to the Chapel of Our Lady of Bethlehem.

The extension of the estate continues, partly due to the project of the Cordoban architect, Arturo Ramirez, supporting Miguel Ángel's desire (another display of magnificence) to embellish this part of the city, demolishing a series of little houses, bought over the last few years, that were built on the remains of the fortress wall that has now been reinstated.

On the way to the library and next to it is the main living room, where we keep all the stud trophies, memorabilia, photos… pictures of the effort and determination of an entire life, of my husband's passion for the Spanish Horse and the Cárdenas lineage.

This living room is located on the first floor of the main facade, the oldest part of the building and the one that has remained since its construction.

Every night I walk through the rooms and "put the house to sleep," first the dogs and then, I look throughout the home and symbolically "tuck her in to bed." I like doing this very much.

I am not very sure whether we have ghosts. I imagine we do. But I am perfectly sure gnomes live among us, little goblins. They are my dachshunds, amusing, humbugs, going in and out from one place to another without stopping, as a living example of perpetual motion.

They are from Lord Bellamy's saga, and were a gift from Rosario my sister-in-law. Lord Richard, Viscount of Bellamy, was a special, intelligent and magnificent dog. He lived with us seventeen years and left an indelible memory. He and his mate, Lady Marjorie, had several children. Honor stayed with us, and then arrived Bellamy's son-in-law from Italy. Named Caruso, he not only distinguished himself by his way of moving, but also with his piercing bark. His daughter and mate is Blondy, fat, fat, but with the most wonderful eyes. They have a two year-old son, an indescribable being that still doesn't know if he is a dog, a person, or a goblin, and goes by the name of Maquroll El Gaviero, in homage and memory of the main character of the author Álvaro Muttis, the Colombian writer I so admire.

We enjoy entertaining and having guests, friends and family. We are very lucky to spend every Christmas in the company of friends. For many years, María Cristine and Michel Denizot, our French family and their children, Jean François, Caroline, Isabel and Frederich, "les enfants que nous partagons," as their mother says, were with us every holiday. They would come with their friends, with their motorbikes, even with their trucks on their way to the desert, their first and last stopover, and like a mini Écija-Dakar, it was amusing.

My cousins, whom we love as siblings, also come: Pablo, Carlos, José Mª, Pilar, and Concha Benavides, their wives, their husbands; the nephews and nieces: Miguel, Pablo, Lourdes, Ana, Inés, María, Balba, Marta, Joaquín, Lucía. Now they bring their own children.

Rosario and Manolo are also with us, along with their children, our nieces, Rosario, Marisol, Macarena, Helen, their husbands, and their children. Although our nieces have their parents' house in Écija, they also bestow their affection on us.

Permanently with us is Miguel Enrile, a nephew, who is not only an efficient assistant but also an ever-entertaining conversationalist. Also Mª José, his wife…

They, and all our friends, Blanca and Fernando Gutiérrez, Baby Gramedo, Lourdes and Bosco Alvear, the San Miguels and their children, Juan in a very special way, Mª Teresa Gudenus today in Australia but always close for us, Alfonso Artaza, Fernanda and Mariano Aguayo, Belén and Alfonso Quintanar, Françoise and Paco González-Camino, Malva Osuna, Blanca and Álvaro Alvear are all part of our life. Each of them has helped to fill our home with pleasant memories.

We have had the honor and the satisfaction of receiving on several occasions H.R.I.H. Don Pedro and Doña Esperanza, Princes of Orleáns, horse lovers of an exceptional human quality.

Painters, writers, Bo Derek, Diandra Douglas, famous photographers of different countries… Robert Vavra, who besides doing this book is, above all, a great friend.

Breeders and friends from America, Marta and Federico Jiménez from Mexico, from the United States Barbara Currie, Eva and José Antonio Cordido Freytes from Venezuela, with his son José Antonio whom we appreciate so much.

We remember those who are no longer with us but have left their immortal memory among these walls. Firstly, our parents, because thanks to them all this has been possible, my brother José Carlos, Aunt Concha, Father Eduardo Huelin, Jesuit friend and spiritual guide, always transmitting peace; Brother Antonio García del Moral with such a great sense of humor; Paco San Miguel, Perico Santaella and Tito Gorostegui.

All will forever remain alive in our hearts.

* * * * * * * * *

During these years, the staff that stays here to help us still shares their time between our house and theirs, accepting the extra work that allows us to entertain and make life pleasant for everybody who comes to us.

The most veteran Chari, cheerful, welcoming, feeding us almost too much; Manuel, her husband who helps me in the garden; Ani and Emilia with the support of Oscar and Marina, their son Oscar Andrés and their baby Josué, born here with us.

Pepe, master carpenter, tireless worker, I can't imagine what would have happened to all of our projects without his effective and superior touch; lattices, doors, Moorish coffered ceilings, restorations, bookcases, and so on, always something new to make. His son Francis has grown admirably, really well indeed, by his side, faithful pupil and his father's admirer and for us somebody very dear.

Rafael the plumber and his electrician son Rafael and so many others have, with so much illusion, helped us continue restoring and improving our home.

And office work… so necessary, all taken care of with effort and proven efficiency by Manolo, for us Manolillo, from his work room, at the San Pablo office.

Houses remain longer than do we… we disappear soon. We put into them, especially in this case, so much energy and so many illusions, so many feelings… Good moments and not so good, hoping that a part of us will remain among the trees and in the ripple of the fountain, so whoever may wander by may listen to the silence and perhaps feel the warmth of our hearts that was left here while we lived.

✳ ✳ ✳ ✳ ✳ ✳ ✳ ✳ ✳

To conclude, I wish to remember Saint Jerome's words of the IInd century in his XIIth epistle to the Galatians:

WE LIVE AS IF WE SHALL DIE TOMORROW, AND WE BUILD AS IF WE SHALL LIVE FOREVER.

A HORSE BREEDER'S REFLECTIONS

I was born seventy years ago in the city of Écija in the province of Seville. My parents belonged to a traditional family of farmers, who inherited agricultural land and livestock from their forebearers.

My father, Miguel Ángel de Cárdenas Llavanera, created a new brand with half of his father-in-law's brand (two yokes together) and half of his father's brand (an anchor), which I have now registered as I will explain further on.

In Andalusia, it is customary for the youngest son to inherit his father's brand, since the first-born or the elder brothers usually leave the parental house earlier and consequently create their own brands. For this reason my father's brand belongs today to my brother Pedro. Since I felt so much affection for my father and for his brand, I was able to keep it, with my brother's approval, adding a 'C' around it, the initial of my surname. With this branding iron I mark my horses, the mares on the outside of the right buttock and the stallions on the left. On the inside of the opposite buttock, under the tail, I mark them with a small iron of my grandfather's brand. I am entitled to use my grandfather's brand as I registered it when my father's youngest brother, who had inherited it, passed away and each of my cousins already had a brand of their own.

My father began to establish the Cárdenas stud during the 1940s. He bought mares from Honorato Jordán, and from the Military Stud descendants of Curro Chica's stock, that is, from the renowned Bocado brand without the 'C.' Later on we encouraged him to buy one of the emblematic sires raised by Roberto Osborne and owned by Fernando Terry. I particularly favored Bilbaíno III since I had seen two of his outstanding sons at the Military Stud. They were Hacendado IV and Gorrón II. The latter floated in the air when in motion.

The problem was that Fernando Terry, patriarch of a family who had an incredible sense of fair play, didn't want to sell either Descarado II or Bílbaíno III. Subsequently my father commissioned an agent, named Manuel Pavón, almost as intelligent and as good a psychologist as my father, to purchase Bílbaíno III for him.

As I have always been known for being somewhat impatient, only a few days had passed when I was already asking Pavón how was it that he had still not bought the horse. "Be silent, my boy," he answered, "I am following the only process that will be fruitful to buy the horse. From time to time, I go to the Terry house when Don Fernando comes to the stables and I constantly praise Descarado II, telling him that he is far better than Bílbaíno

III." And this is how he finally managed to buy Bílbaíno III, or at least that is how he told me he had achieved it.

When my father passed away, we continued together under the name of Widow and Sons of Miguel Ángel Cárdenas. Later, when my mother died, we still remained together for several years as Sucessors of Miguel Ángel Cárdenas. In 1987, my brother and I decided to divide the horses. I formed two shares and we made a draw. After that I bought quite a few horses from my brother from his allotment.

Before my father died, two of Bilbaíno III sons were chosen for studs. They were Vassallo II and Valido, both of such exceptional quality that they won many prizes in competitions and produced countless beautiful and outstanding offspring.

I also have to mention the sires from the Military Stud that refreshed our bloodlines and produced offspring with an improved athletic performance. They were Levitón, Jenson and Evento. I should also name Poseído III who was the sire of our Champion of Spain, Genil.

Genil was of pure Carthusian lines, and there is a story about him that is particularly moving. I have traveled many times to the United States, Mexico and other countries of America and Europe as part of the Pure Bred Spanish Horse Grading Committee. On one of my trips to Mexico, after traveling several days all over the country, we went to the south, to the farm of Federico Jiménez Sainz in the State of Tabasco, near Villahermosa. This breeder had convinced me to sell him Genil, but only after many phone calls and having accepted considerable increases in the horse's price.

The day I went with the Grading Committee to visit his farm, we watched an exhibition of Federico's magnificent horses. At the end of it, as a finale, Genil was let loose and gave a wonderful performance... trotting, rearing and pirouetting. Meanwhile, a musical tune that became very popular during the 1992 Expo of Seville was being played. When Genil passed in front of where we were sitting, he suddenly stopped, came toward me, and with his muzzle started to caress my legs that were at the same height as his head. I couldn't contain my tears. And I believe that many of those who witnessed the horse's behavior also cried. This happening occurred eight years after the horse was sold and had left Spain for Mexico.

As for the horses of pure Carthusian lines, Juan Carlos Altamirano carried out a praiseworthy study of archives for years and years that separated the real history from the invented fantasies.

Bilbaíno III was a sire on my farm for twelve years, and his sons Vassallo II and Valido were also with me for as long as he had been. Most important, they sired exceptionally uniform offspring. This uniformity may also be seen in the *cobras* (groups of mares) that are composed of almost identical-appearing females. The word *cobra* (to receive payment in Spanish) originates from the time when the farmers who didn't have mares, or not enough, to thresh the wheat with their hoofs, would bring in mares from other farms, paying for the service. This resulted in the expression: "Bring in the cobras." (Bring in the ones that receive payment – that is, the hired mares.) As for the quality of our farm, it is enough to say that this stud won the largest number of prizes during the 60s and 70s – that is, during the last three decades of the 20th century and the beginning of the 21st. This homogeneity remains even with the new bloodlines of the Military Stud horses that have genetic backgrounds without pure Carthusian blood.

Recently I bought the stallion Fuego XII, whose movements and good disposition for dressage reveal an outstanding potential. I also bought his sire, Utrerano VII, who is of excellent quality.

At the SICAB, the most important Spanish Horse show in the world, I showed a group of twenty-one mares in hand with only one man and his assistant working them. At this exhibition when the organizers of Equitana, the largest equestrian trade fair in the world that includes all sorts of breeds, saw the mares' performance, they invited me to show them at their event. It was a very big success. After that I have continued showing groups of mares at SICAB and at other exhibitions.

I am touched when I remember some of the previous chairmen of our association, those who did not hesitate choosing for a show a judge who had not given any prizes to the chairman's horses. They were living examples of correctness and honesty.

I have to mention the judges who qualify for the 'Feria del Campo' and until recently for the Championship of Spain, because they were very professional and unbiased. With those impartial judges, my stud won many prizes. Vasallo II was Overall Champion in the 'Feria del Campo' in 1972 and Best Overall Champion in the Jerez Horse Fair in 1978. Valido also was Overall Champion in the last organized 'Feria del Campo' in 1975 and won the Championship of Spain organized by AECE in 1983. Both Vasallo and Valido have left countless offspring, sons and grandsons that have been winners. A son of Valido was Juguetón V, Best Overall Champion in the Jerez Horse Fair in 1982. Gastador VIII, also Valido's son, was Champion of Spain in 1985 and in SICAB in 1991. A son of Gastador VIII, and therefore grandson of Valido, is Unguido IV, three times Champion of Andalusia and Champion of Spain in 1995. Clásico MAC, also a son of Gastador VIII, was Champion of Spain in 2000 and 2001.

It is always a pity to sell good horses but, with the exception of certain stallions that have to be kept, a stud farm has to alternate its own breeding stock. I once sold a well trained stallion to Manuel Bertolín that he, in turn, sold because someone offered a very good price for the horse. This made his daughter, Fátima, very unhappy because she had become extremely attached to the horse. She insisted that her father buy her another horse of the same brand and with the same level of training. Bertolín, concerned by his daughter's sadness, phoned me requesting a horse to substitute for the one he had sold. Unfortunately I didn't have that horse, but by chance, I had just received the *Equestrian Magazine* and on the front cover was a picture of Gastador VIII that I had sold when he was two years old. The picture, taken on the beach in Valencia, showed the horse ridden by a very good rider. I told Bertolín to have a look at the magazine and encouraged him to buy the horse, which he did. Later, because of his generosity, he let me have the horse to show as one of my sires. It was then that Gastador won the Gold Medal and Championship of Spain in 1985. It was easy to imagine the father's and daughter's happiness. Later on, I exchanged the horse with them for a pair of driving horses and once again, this time as its real owner, I presented him in SICAB 91. And again he won the Gold Medal and Championship of Spain.

At the end of the 80s, the African horse disease spread throughout Spain and became epidemic. It was caused by a group of imported horses that had made a stopover in Africa, and ended up in Sotogrande after passing via Madrid. The association and breeders thought that in a year or so the disease would be eradicated. But perhaps due to a certain lack of authority and to some negligent owners, horses were moved around spreading the epidemic from the Club de Campo and Puerta de Hierro in Madrid to the big breeding farms in Andalusia.

The absolute immobility of horses was imposed by law. I was part of a group of breeders who invited to Spain a specialist from South Africa, where the disease was endemic. We finally were able to have a vaccination program approved by the Spanish Animal Health Authorities, but it still took four years to officially declare Spain free from the disease.

As nobody would have guessed that it would take so long to eradicate the epidemic, I continued covering mares and after four unfortunate years of quarantine, I had far too many horses in my stable. I then held an auction at my stud farm with an extensive advertising campaign, not only in Spain, but also in United States, Mexico and other countries – which attracted a large attendance. We even sold some horses over the phone. The economic situation of the stud farm was thus improved when more than 50 horses were sold at very good prices.

Horse breeding in Spain has improved tremendously with regard to nutrition, health and training. We are already competing in dressage with very good results, in part because our knowledge of equine health is far better than it was some years ago.

When the Spanish Horse Breeder's Association was founded in Seville in May 1972, I was named treasurer. This association, as many others that have been established, has been very successful in promoting the Spanish Horse.

In Europe and on other continents, we have witnessed efforts made by the Spanish Horse breeders. I have very often been a member of the Pure Bred Spanish Horse Grading Committee and have become great friends with many of the Spanish Horse Committee staff, especially with Lieutenant Colonel José Bobi Miguel. Our breed is known as the Spanish Horse, not the Andalusian – this word for our horse is used by breeders here who are naturally proud that a breed that originates here has spread throughout the world with the name Spanish.

The Spanish Horse owes so much to a number of breeders for their troubles and sacrifices. Perfect gentlemen, honest and generous who have dedicated their lives to preserve such a beautiful breed. I must mention the late dearly-missed Paco Lazo, Gentleman of the Order of the Agricultural Merit, loyal, sincere, and a very great friend of mine. Almost every day we spoke to each other on the phone. I also have the honor of Francisco Fernández-Daza's friendship, a pleasant, honest, distinguished gentleman from Extremadura, and there are others: Alfonso, Marquis of Quintanar, intelligent Castilian breeder and admirable friend; Paco Montaño who helped me so much while I was president of the Seville Association; César Alba who has succeeded me in the presidency of this association and son of the president of the ACCE, Paco Alba, and others.

It is also necessary to name some exceptional people from other countries: Barbara Currie, from United States, founder and president of the Foundation for the Spanish Horse, wonderful organizer and outstanding with everything that surrounds her; in México, Federico Jiménez Sainz, Abelardo Morales, Antonio Ariza; in Costa Rica, Tomás Batalla; in Venezuela, José Antonio Cordido Freytes.

I suppose, at this moment, I have forgotten to mention so many, many other friends who have made such an important effort to promote the Spanish Horse. I hope they will forgive me for my lack of memory.

However, I cannot forget to point out the company and help that for years I have had from my nephew Miguel Enrile Osuna, who is not only fond of the horses but a tireless worker as well.

Of my staff at the stud and the farms (orange trees, cotton, and so on), I want to mention Manuel Martínez Blanca, manager of the company's main office who is in charge of all the accounts and is so dedicated that he hardly ever takes a holiday.

Antonio Calvo Aguilera, who has worked for me since he was a young boy, is a determined horseman and senior of all the stud staff. José Joaquín Cabrera León is in charge of the Saetilla Farm who, together with my nephew Miguel and the technical engineers, supervise the crop and the irrigation systems. We are also fortunate to have the assistance of the veterinary surgeon Juan Galisteo.

I shall not continue as the list is endless. Again, I hope that those not mentioned will also pardon me.

Not very long ago, I sold Vándalo, trained for dressage at Grand Prix Level, to Diandra Douglas. At this time my wife Carmen and some friends and I visited Diandra one weekend at 'La Estaca,' her house in Mallorca. One afternoon while we were there, we went to visit Pedro Salas, an important breeder and also founder of our Association. At this time Pedro told us a story I must relate.

"With a group of friends," said Pedro Salas, "I was examining all the horses on exhibition at a horse show. I was really putting all my attention into it, probably getting in everybody's way and annoying the stud managers and grooms. When we came to a group of mares that really impressed me, I began to tell my friends how good these mares were, when somebody behind my back asked who I was. At the time I was considered to be a well-known person who was President of the County Council. 'I'm just examining the horses,' I replied to him. 'You are getting in the way,' he told me. Then he asked, 'So, what do you think of these mares?' 'They are the best,' I answered. The man was Miguel Ángel Cárdenas Llavaneras. After this we had a long conversation and became such friends that he gave me one of the mares as a gift." Pedro Salas also added that he had never heard a negative comment from anybody about my father, which understandably filled me with joy.

I have been very fond of horses since I was a small boy and, when I was studying away from Écija, every time I spoke to my father on the phone I tired him out with all my questions about horses. I was always curious to know the foals that had been born, and which of the sires was going to cover each of the mares; then I would give him my opinion. Usually he would follow it – because it would coincide with his own.

As years have gone by, my fondness for horses has turned into such a passion that I could not envision life without them.

PHOTO ALBUM

UNGIDO (*Lemos*)

Miguel Ángel Cárdenas Llavanera at the Club
Pineda of Seville.

Miguel Ángel Cárdenas Osuna riding Valido.

His Royal Majesty (then Prince of Spain) giving Miguel Ángel a prize.

Carmen and Miguel Ángel at the Championship of Spain in the Club Pineda of Seville.

His Royal Majesty, The King of Spain with a Cárdenas Horse.

Cobra of mares at Equitana (Essen, Germany).

Miguel Ángel with his nephew and second in charge Miguel Enrile.

Carmen, Bo Derek, Miguel Ángel and Miguel Enrile at San Pablo.

Bo and Miguel Ángel at San Pablo.

Robert Vavra, Miguel Ángel, Bo and architect Paco González-Camino.

Michael and Diandra Douglas with Miguel Ángel at San Pablo.

Keanu Reeves with Miguel Ángel at San Pablo.

H.R.H. Princes Doña Esperanza and Don Pedro of Orléans with Carmen and Miguel Ángel at San Pablo.

Miguel Ángel at Federico Jiménez's house in Tabasco (México) with Genil.

MÁSTIL *(Lemos)*

EPILOGUE

In early 1974 my fascination for the horse and my interest in equitation took me to Jerez de la Frontera, my father's family's native city. At that time, the Andalusian School of Equestrian Art was formed because of Alvaro Domecq's great passion for the project. He started only with a small number of horsemen and the support of his friends. After the presentation of the show "How Spanish Horses Dance" at Jerez's Fair of the Horse, Alvaro Domecq received the "Golden Horse Award." Then it became obvious that concentrated training had to continue because of the performances that had been booked in European countries as well as for the exhibitions that regularly took place in a provisional riding hall. It was then that I became part of the Jerez Riding School to organize the daily training and to instruct the new riders.

Just as any performance has its main actors, the stars of Alvaro's show were two horses of Miguel Ángel Cárdenas, Vendaval and Veneno. Those two horses, together with Vasallo, all sons of Bilbaíno III, had won the prize for Best Lot of three-year-old stallions in the 1970 Feria del Campo of Madrid.

The limited number of horses prepared at the time to perform in Alvaro's entire exhibition meant that they had to be able to go into the show ring several times a day to execute demanding high school exercises. Those stallions, without a doubt, were exceptional horses.

Veneno was a stunning horse with true-to-type features and spectacular movement. He led the final carousel and his entrance in the ring always elicited the public's applause. Pictured *shoulders-in* with his astounding mane, for years he was featured on the show promotional poster.

Vendaval was the prodigious artist. I don't think I have known a horse with such a good disposition for work. After having overcome several serious illnesses, including tetanus, his spirit and his heart continued even more energetically to demonstrate his limitless abilities for any exercise. His *levades* and *caprioles* were the highlight of many exhibitions.

Having known these horses, it is easy to understand why classic authors praised the Spanish Horses for their docility and excellence. Cárdenas' horses fit to perfection any one of those famous quotes. As La Guerinière said: "All the authors have given preference to the Spanish Horse"… "It is a breed worthy of conserving, selecting and enhancing." So the horses of Cárdenas' origin have been selected for years, proving that the qualities of the Spanish Horse continue today more vibrant and vigorous than they did several centuries ago.

Selection in breeding horses does not happen by

chance but is due to the persistence, as well as the consistancy and the wisdom of those who profoundly know these animals. This can only be appreciated by the expert observer who understands the customs and roots of his country and knows the road he has followed and that toward which he is aiming. Clearly a Spanish Horse is much more than an animal, it is a part of our history and our culture: a history that Miguel Ángel's wife Carmen, with her knowledge of Éjica's development, has reconstructed with success and expertise as she so skillfully describes this remarkable city's transition from past to present.

The history of Vasallo II is also extraordinary. After winning the Gold Medal for three-year-old stallions in 1970, he was proclaimed Champion so many times that not only has he been the highest winning Spanish Horse, but his progeny have also obtained more prizes than any other stallions of the breed. He is the sire with the highest score in the Book of Merits of the Breed. Vasallo II,

Valido, Genil, Gastador VIII, Ungido IV and Clásico, offspring of Bilbaíno III, have won nine Championships of Spain and three Championships of Andalusia.

If the endless list of trophies of the Cárdenas Stud is more than brilliant, still more satisfying for a breeder is for one of his horses, in this case Fuego XII, to be selected for the dressage team that will represent Spain in the World Championship and the next Olympic Games. This was due to the magnificent scores obtained by Fuego XII in dressage competitions, demonstrating that presently the Spanish Horses of Cárdenas origin are even more alive and active than ever.

More important than all the achievements is the satisfaction, the beauty, and the happiness that the Cárdenas stallions and mares have brought to the world's many horse lovers who have had the opportunity of owning, riding, caring for, stroking, or simply admiring these exceptional and unique horses.

— *Mercedes González Cort*

ACKNOWLEDGEMENTS

First, in the name of all the photographers who have enjoyed and benefited from the hospitality and help of Miguel Ángel Cárdenas, I extend to him our deepest thanks. Miguel Ángel has always been willing to go beyond normal shooting situations to provide us photographers with unique opportunities to capture his stallions in action or repose. This is not only evidenced by the pictures in this book which depict the Spanish Horses in images not seen before on the printed page, but by the reality that his stallions have appeared on the covers of at least half a dozen books. No other breeder of Spanish Horses in the world has been so honored.

Photo by Leni Riefenstahl

Robert Vavra

Next I wish to thank Miguel Ángel's wife, Carmen, for her extremely gracious hospitality to my crew as day after day and night after night we photographed the Cárdenas house and grounds.

Always present to help with logistics or whatever it was to make our work easier and more successful was Miguel Ángel's nephew Miguel Enrile. I hope by now his Siamese fighting fish has produced offspring because of the female Beta I encouraged him to acquire.

My work for this book was happily made easier because of my dedicated assistant, Juan Manuel del Valle, who never faltered during our many days in Écija and of driving back and forth between there and Seville. Juanma's presence greatly enriched my life and work, and he will always have my deepest thanks for his contribution to this project. For recommending him, I thank my good friend, Emilio Saenz.

Wayne Chasan I first met seventeen years ago when he photographed my ranch in Seville for a magazine. Wayne is as intense in his work as I am in mine and was always willing to make the extra effort and take the extra four rolls of film to capture the Cárdenas house in the way I felt it should be shown. In between the hard work and long hours, we had good laughs and enjoyed a true feeling of camaraderie. Important to any success this book might enjoy was the presence of Wayne's assistant José Sánchez Marín. Together they were always ready to make reality on film the images I envisioned in my mind.

For three book projects I have counted on the creative expertise and talent of Travis Smith with whom I have spent hours, days, weeks, and months making sure that each of the images in this book would hopefully realize its potential. Travis was always willing to go "the extra mile" and was not only invaluable in my work, but his presence was a continued source of happiness. In fact, with Trav, I enjoyed the kind of camaraderie which has not been my experience since I was ten years old.

Once more I thank my great friend Victor Diaz and The International Institute of Photographic Arts for their support with this project, especially the scanning of all the images that appear here. An added treat whenever possible was the company of Victor's wife Marta and daughter Jessica.

Irving Rubin, also of IIPA, will never know how valuable his sage advice and friendship have been to me and this project. I can never thank Irv enough for his support, especially during some very difficult moments with the production of this book. Irv's wife Sandra also brought joy into this project.

At IIPA I would also like to thank Victor Gallardo.

Mercedes González Cort has my special thanks for doing the translation of this book and for continuing to be a very special part of my life. Taking time from life and work as one of Spain's most esteemed international judges of Spanish Horses, Mercedes spent long hours on this book. Along with that of Candela, her lovely daughter, Mercedes' voice was usually heard from Spain at 6 a.m. California time.

As with my last two books, *Horses of the Sun* and *Stallions of the Quest*, I entrusted the printing of *Cárdenas: Horses and Home* to South Sea International Press in Hong Kong. There I would especially like to thank Franky Ho and George Lo for their high level of professionalism and for their friendship.

My deepest gratitude and that of Miguel Ángel Cárdenas goes to Tomas Miček, Till Leeser, and Thomas Kilper for allowing their splendid images to appear in these pages. We also thank Rafael Lemos and Liza Kellner for their images.

For their help with this project, I thank especially Ray Volcama of Colorado Studios, as well as my old friend Phil Garvin. For the editing of these pages I thank Carol Cramer, Gale Vavra and Janey Parkinson.

Sirkka Huovila and Sally Stein have my gratitude for the typing of these words. I also thank Sirkka's husband, Ismo, for his assistance. To John Dixon I am indebted for introducing me to Travis and Sirkka.

For support during the seven months it took to do this book, I thank David and Lee Black, Ted Purpero, and especially Ron and Gale Vavra.

Once more I counted on the dedication and skill of Mary Weldy, my production assistant. Mary's husband, Bob, also provided sound advice.

These words would be incomplete without thanks to that extraordinary artist Mariano Aguayo and also to Ursula Schöfer for her help.

Most important are my profound thanks to the men and women of the Cárdenas breeding farm and home for their continued assistance and hard work to make this project happen. I would like to thank the expert rider Juan Manuel Muñoz Díaz. At the ranch of San Pablo and at the Cárdenas home we had the good fortune to count on the tireless effort of the staff who are pictured later in this book, along with my own production team.

Lastly for their patience and great effort, I extend my deepest appreciation and affection to Vasallo, Mástil, Fuego, Junco, Ecuador, Genil, Clásico, Vandalo, Gitano, as well as to the more than eighty Cárdenas mares who so brilliantly display their beauty in the pages of this book.

PHOTOGRAPHERS
HOME & RANCH STAFF
PRODUCTION TEAM
ABOUT THE AUTHOR

Wayne Chasan

Thomas Kilper

With his inspired vision, Wayne Chasan imbues magic and emotion into the spectacular homes which he has photographed over the last twenty years.

It is Wayne's innate ability to capture and create mood, combined with his masterful use of the photographer's palette of light, form, texture and composition that makes his images so powerful.

An American based in Andalucia, his work earned him Spain's prestigious LUX Gold Award and is often featured in publications worldwide, including *Elle*, *Décor* and *Vogue*. Wayne's intimate photographs of traditional Andalucia have been exhibited in New York and Spain.

Born in Germany, Thomas Kilper studied photography, after which he traveled the world working with other cameramen. He has been a professional photographer for seventeen years and his clients include Hugo Boss, Escada, Siemens, BMW, Mercedes Benz, Lufthansa, and others.

Horses are his passion and he loves to ride. His first book project was *The Spanish Horse* in which he captured equines with all their natural beauty and elegance, drawing on his experience as a fashion photographer. "I attempted to find the beauty in horses much as when I am photographing fashion models," says Thomas. And judging from his images he has indeed succeeded.

Tomas Miček

Till Leeser

Tomas Miček was born in Moravian Ostrau, Czechoslovakia. After graduating from the University in Brünn with a doctorate in geography, he originally intended to pursue a scientific career, but then discovered photography. So, he dropped his profession and followed his calling.

Tomas' work has also appeared in *Stern*, *GEO*, *FAZ*, *Vogue*, *L'Europeo*, *The Observer*, *Argosy*, *Nou*, as well as in other publications.

Tomas Miček has specialized in the photography of horses, having done a dozen beautiful books on them. For years he has had a great love for Andalusians, also photographing other breeds: Camargue, Haflinger, Norwegian and Icelandic horses, Lipizzaners, Friesians, and Arabians. His books also feature Greece and Alpine forests.

Till Leeser was born in Schweinfurt, Germany, in 1949. He studied at the Folkwangschule in Essen. Later he worked in Paris as a freelance photographer. Presently he lives in Hamburg where he taught at Fachhochschule, Hamburg. He was a founder of the photographers' archive Bilderburg and a member of the Art Directors' Club Deutschland.

Till Leeser's photographs have appeared in the advertisements for Alfa Romeo, Audi, British Airways, DaimlerChrysler, Saab, Toyota, and BMW. His black and white equine images in these pages are from his splendid book *Por las Sendas del Caballo de Pura Raza Española*. They appear here through the courtesy of the book's publisher, Siruela of Madrid.

Miguel Enrile Osuna
Nephew and Personal Assistant

Arturo Ramirez
Home Architect

SAN PABLO STAFF

Juan Galisteo
Veterinarian

Manuel Martínez Blanca
Office

Manuel Corzo Rodríguez
Office

Antonio Calvo Aguilera
Senior Rider

Daniel Pérez Calvo
Cobra

Juan Manuel Priego Gómez

Nicolás Calvo Postigo

José Ramón Tirado García

HOUSE STAFF

Rosario Jiménez Escalera

Ana Martín Villegas

Oscar Anzules Merchan

Marina Guaraca Guaraca

Emilia Martin

José Rosado Morón
Carpenter

Francisco Rosado Borja
Carpenter

Manuel Borja
Gardener

PRODUCTION TEAM

Juan Manuel del Valle
Vavra Assistant

Jose Sánchez Marín
Chasan Assistant

Travis Smith
Creative Assistant

Charles Chiarello
Equivision

Mary L. Weldy
Production Assistant

Carol Cramer
Editor

Mary Jane Parkinson
Editor

Sirkka Huovila
Typist

Mercedes González Cort
Translations

Mercedes was born in Madrid and educated in England, France and Spain. She has been First Rider and Teacher at the Andalusian School of Equestrian Art and the only Spanish woman to ride in the Spanish Riding School of Vienna. She is an experienced Master of Classical Dressage and Academic Equitation. Mercedes is an Official Judge of the Spanish Breeding Authorities and a great expert on the Pure Bred Spanish Horse, traveling throughout the world to judge and to spread the knowledge of the breed. She is an honorary member of El Club del Caballo Español and of the Academic Forum of Equestrian Studies.